# TOLEDO

## ...ART AND

## ...HISTORY

**BY: RUFINO MIRANDA**
**TRANSLATED BY: MARGARET McCLAFFERTY**

# *Toledo*

## INTRODUCTION

Two thousand years have passed since the name of Toledo entered recorded history. The Roman historian, Titus Livius, mentioned Toledo in his descriptions of the doings of Marcus Fulvius, who conquered the city at the head of the Roman legions. He wrote: "Toletum, ibi parva urbis erat, set loco munito".

Much has been written about the city since then. In the attempt to decipher the palimpsest of the civilizations which have left their mark on the city, poets, archaeologists, philosophers, historians and even theologians have investigated its every aspect, casting light on its most secret places and describing its monuments.

For centuries, wise men and artists have tried to solve the enigma of this multi-cultural city. It has been the meeting place for many different

*Panoramic view*

races, a melting pot of ideas and the birthplace of original culture. However, like all places with a special destiny, Toledo jealously guards one final secret, one not written in any book, and which is only revealed by personal experience.

To enjoy the experience of Toledo is not comparable to turning the pages of a history book, as the city is not a mere chapter in the history of Spain: it is the expression of Spanish history itself.

This book is neither a work of investigation, nor does it set out new theories or hypotheses to explain matters already studied and verified.

Some books written on the subject of Toledo have already become classics. However, they are useful only as works of reference, hard to come across and difficult to read. Others are specialized monographs, long, detailed and useless for the rushed modern tourist. On the other hand, there are the books designed for sale as souvenirs, which are full of colourful pictures and contain little information.

The author tries to fill the gap between these two extremes with this book. In the first instance, he wishes to complete and modernize all investigations carried out to date and, as the aim of this guide is to cover all that can be seen in one long day's visit, he has limited himself to what is accessible in that period of time. He has also taken care to portray the historical context of each of the monuments he describes, in order to make its creation and the reason for its existence more understandable.

This book is like a ray of light, an aid to the traveller, and later is of help in refreshing his memory.

One must go through the conventual quarter, set apart from mundane bustle in the silvery silence of the night, whispering so as not to break the silence, which is broken only by the monastic bell. At dawn, from the other side of the river valley, one must contemplate how the sun gilds the polychromatic ochre shades of the bricks, or the grey granite of the large porches. One must lose oneself in the ruggedness of the streets when, at sunset, the city slackens its pace, and the powers of magic flow forth.


Deciphering Toledo is an intimate and personal experience.


RUFINO MIRANDA,
Christmas, 1988.

# NEW BISAGRA GATE

Emperor Charles V decided to improve the appearance of the city by enlarging and remodelling the Alcázar palace, while at the same time giving the city a suitable main gate.

The gullies and rough patches on the road to Madrid had already been smoothed out when Parliament was held in Toledo in 1538. **Nicolás de Vergara the older** was given the job of renovating the old medieval city gate. While he respected the bases of the twin towers, he remodelled the room used by the gate keeper.

The architect **Alonso de Covarrubias** later went on to extend the space within the gate to create an extensive courtyard. He also designed the facade which can be seen nowadays, and added the a semicircular towers on each side of the central Gateway. These are in dressed stone, on which a fine imperial shield in granite stands out, surmounted by a double - headed eagle.

Although the commemorative stone plaque here states that work on the gate finished in 1550, at a time when four generations of the royal family were alive (Juana la loca (Joan the mad), Charles the emperor, his son the future Philip II and the unfortunate prince Carlos), it is known that a final stage of works was undertaken around 1575. It was then that **Nicolás de Vergara the younger** added a second level onto the Arab towers, completing them with spires of glazed tiles. He also sculpted the image of Saint Eugenio.

**The Bisagra Gate** lies on the natural route into the city, at what has always been its most accessible point. This is where it gives onto the northern plain, called the **"Sagra"** by the Arabs because of the reddish colour of its soil, and still known by the same name.

It can therefore be seen that, in spite of the numerous controversies which have taken place over the years as to the origins of the name of this gate, it is none other than **"Bab - Sagra"**, i.e., the Sagra Gate.

When the gate was undergoing cleaning in 1968, a piece of stone with an incomplete cufic inscription was found. It contains the name of Imael Al - Zafir (1032 - 1044) who founded the Toledan Taifa (one of the regions into which Spain was divided on the fall of the Cordoban Caliphate). He was the father of the famous Al -Mamún. If this stone is related to the construction of the original gate, then it must date from the VI century.

The fact that the two gates are hardly 80 metres apart has given rise to much controversy, as to which of them is the original Bisagra Gate. These have never been satisfactorily resolved. The gate described above is generally known as the Puerta Nueva (New Gate), while the old gate has been renamed the Puerta de **Alfonso VI**, as it is thought that he passed under it on the victorious entry of Christian troops into the city on its reconquest, on the 25th of May, 1085.

*Bisagra Gate*

## THE OLD BISAGRA GATE OR ALFONSO VI GATE

This is certainly the city gate which has suffered fewest alterations, and still has an almost completely original facade. This is due to its being covered for many years after the new gate was opened during the times of Charles V.

The originality of this gate, in a well defended angle of the walls with two additional flanking towers, next to the "Macbora" (cemetery) means that it must have once been the main gate of the city, and could hardly have been a side or less important gate.

The proportions and stone work of its horse shoe arch date it as being X century. A floral carving on the key stone of the arch dates from Visigoth times. The strangest feature of this gate is the lintel, the presence of which has never been satisfactorily explained.

A blocked up side gate can be seen in the tower on the right, while the upper parts are XIII century Mudejar work, as can be seen from the bricks and style of the building work.

In 1905 the gate was cleaned, and the side nearest the city demolished to create an attractive courtyard. It is to be hoped that considerations of taste and respect will eventually bring about the removal of a modern "sculpture" placed here.

*Alfonso VI Gate*

## THE PUERTA DEL SOL (SUN GATE)

The steep hill up into the city through the **Bab-al-Mardum** (Gate of Cristo de la Luz) is impassible for wagons and tiring for horses. It was therefore necessary to lay out another easier route following the line of the city wall. The entrance to this new way up into the city is through the **Puerta del Sol.**

In spite of its position outside and perpendicular to the wall, it is nonetheless a true entrance into the city.

It was built during the times of Archbishop Tenorio (1375 - 1399). It is thought to be the finest Mudejar style gate in Spain, combining strength and harmonious lines.

The round towers are built in rubble work, and the matching pointed and horse-shoe shaped arches in are granite. The decorative work of the two sets of arches, the parapets and battlements, and the inside of the gate are in brick. This combination of building materials is very common in Mudejar work.

A medallion containing a triangle showing the ordination of Saint Idelfonso was placed above the horseshoe arch in the XVI century. Many years later a sun and moon were painted on either side of the medallion, and thus about two hundred years ago the gate ceased being known as the **"Gate of the Blacksmith's"**, being renamed "The Puerta del Sol" ("Gate of the Sun").

There is a small window in the first frieze of interlocking arches. This was used for carrier pigeons. Under this window is a marble embossing taken from a paleochristian sarcophagus. It shows the denial of Saint Peter.

*Detail of the sixteenth century medallion*

12   *The Gate of the Sun*

# THE CAMBRON GATE

**The Cambrón Gate** stands In the walls that run from the Old Bisagra Gate to San Martin Bridge. It is located at the place where a very large water course runs out of the city during rains, and must therefore date from the earliest times.

It has been identified as the Bab al - Yahud, or Gate of the Jews. This city gate is often mentioned in documents from the XII century onwards, and gave entrance to the populous Jewish quarter of the city.

Part of the original structure is still conserved in the outer part of the gate, in the form of the opening with a square tower at either side. In the base of these towers can be seen two large Arab memorial stones, taken from the nearby cemetery. On one of these stones the original inscription can still be seen.

The gate suffered a complete transformation during general reforms undertaken during the second half of the XVI century. Work on the gate was directed by Nicolas de Vergara the younger.

Two new towers were added to the gate, making it symmetrical and creating a small internal courtyard. The first floor of the gate house was renovated so that it could be used as living quarters for the gate keeper and guards. The facade was changed, and the shield of the Royal family added. A beautiful sculpture by Berruguete of Saint Leocardia, martyr and patron of the city, was placed inside the gate.

The Gate still has its old iron - covered doors. In 1577 the Queen granted the city the special privilege of not having to shut these every night.

The name "Cambrón" (hawthorn) first appeared during the middle of the XV century. The origins of this name are obscure, although it could come from the hawthorn trees which used to grow in abundance around the gate, while one of them even took root in one of the towers.

Not far from the gate a rectangular tower stands out over the wall. Among the granite stones of which it is built, others of limestone can be seen, these latter being of Visigoth origin. This is known as the Torre de los Abades (Abotts' Tower) as it was valiantly defended by Archbishop Don Bernardo and his canons during the Almoravid invasions, which took place between 1090 and 1099.

*Cambrón Gate*

# SAN JUAN DE LOS REYES

This fine church ("Saint John of the Kings") lies just a bowshot from the Cambrón Gate. It is built on an area of relatively flat land in the Jewish quarter. From the viewing platform just in front of the church there is a view of the hills and houses ("Cigaralles") on the other side of the river and the plain of the Vega. The church is surmounted by an octagonal dome and flanked by buttresses.

The origins of this church go back to the Battle of Toro, in 1476, between followers of the Beltraneja family and those faithful to the young princess Isabel and prince Ferdinand. This battle decided the succession of the Throne of Castile.

Victory in the battle went to the Royal couple, and to crown the occasion Isabel decided to build a monastery as a votive temple and Royal pantheon.

The **architect** - sculptor was Hans Waas (a name rendered Juan Guas in Spanish). He was born in a village in Brittany, Saint - Paul de León, and came to Toledo while still a child with his father, Pedro. They came as Pedro was a member of the group of sculptors who travelled with Hanequin of Brussels. The boy was brought up and educated in Toledo, where he eventually married a girl from Torrijos, Marina Alverez. His education as a sculptor culminated in his work on the Door of the Lions of the Cathedral, working with the group of Flemish sculptors entrusted with the work.

He worked in a luminous style, although his roots and artistic vocabulary were founded in Toledo. San Juan de los Reyes is therefore in a gothic style, although it draws inspiration from the core of the local Mudejar style.

The **church:** This has a single aisle composed of four sections of extremely complex vaulting. There is a Royal Gallery above the columns which give access to the transept. The stonework here is better described in terms of fine jewellery than those of stone masonry.

Around the Royal Gallery run the initials of the royal names, F and Y, finishing in a fretwork parapet.

The **walls of the Presbytery** which was to have housed the royal tombs are decorated in the most lavish style. Never has the rhythmic repetition of a heraldic design given rise to a decorative effect of such beauty.

The church is dedicated to Saint John, and his eagle holds the royal shields in its talons. These are flanked by the yoke and arrows.

There may be other, purer examples of the gothic, but none that is richer or more amazing.

The **screen behind the altar**. The original, together with the stalls and library, was destroyed during the sacking which the church suffered during the Napoleonic wars. The one now in place is by Francisco de Comontes, and was brought here from the Santa Cruz Hospital. Its origins are shown by the shields of the Mendoza family which it contains.

Above the screen behind the altar is a beautiful painting showing "The Allegory of the Defense of the Dogma of the Conception", painted by Romero Carrión, an artist who died young, in 1967.

The **cloisters.** When Juan Guas died in 1496, his co-workers, the Egas brothers, carried on with the construction of the cloisters, which were finished in 1504.

*The Upper cloisters*

*The retable of St. John of the Kings*

The harmony of proportion to be found in its broad windows is emphasized by the extremely fine mullions, and is enhanced by the fretwork decoration, which attains the delicacy of lace. A set of statues lines the four galleries.

The windows of the **upper cloister** are in a mixed (curved - straight - curved) style. They are the personal creation of Guas, while the roof is multicoloured woodwork and was a later addition.

The door in the outside wall of the cloisters was added at a much later date. It follows a design by Covarrubias (1610) and is not worthy of the building as a whole.

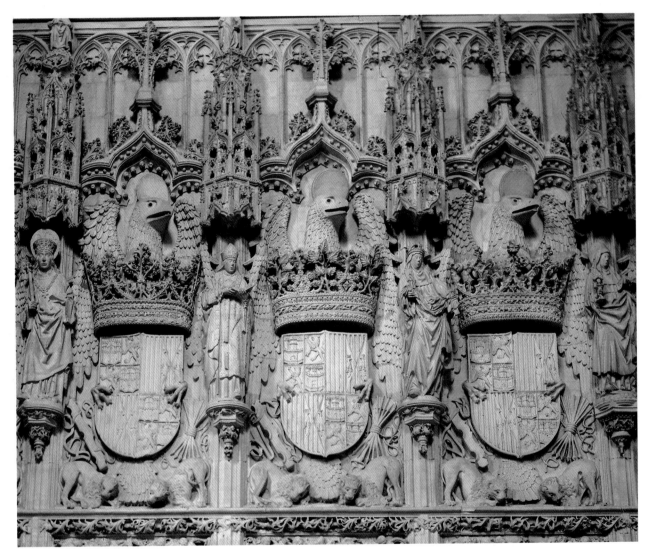

*St. John of the Kings: Church*

The chains and manacles of Christians once held prisoner hang from the granite walls. These prisoners were released during the gradual conquest of the forts and castles of the Nazarí kingdom, a process which culminated in the surrender of Granada on the 2 - I - 1492.

*Lower cloister*

# CLOISTERS

*Panelling*

## SANTA MARIA LA BLANCA SYNAGOGUE

Of the ancient splendour of the Toledo Synagogues, the richest and most prestigious of all those within the Sepharad, only two still stand. The memory of another lives on in a street name.

Many theories have grown around the beautiful and original synagogue now known as Santa Maria la Blanca ("Saint Mary the White"). These theories are attempts to date the building, as well as explaining its liturgical purpose and artistic style.

Some believe that this is the building constructed by Jusef ben Jossan (d. 1205) the tax collector of Alfonso VIII. Others state that it is the synagogue known as "Al Malikin" or Abu - DARHAM, and date it from the end of the XIII century, its construction having been paid for by David ben Solomón ben Abi - Durham (d. 1270).

The system of illumination used in this building in antiquity has never been satisfactorily explained: the bulls - eye windows which can be seen nowadays are a relatively recent addition. One theory is that originally the roofs of the aisles sloped down on each side from their centres, thereby allowing light to enter inside the building through what are now blind windows.

The **main facade** was the East wall, in which the small blocked up entrance door may be seen.

Nor is there any certainty as to where the ladies' gallery was located. One theory is that the building used to be longer, reaching into what is now the garden. This would explain the beams incorporated in the base of what is now the main door, as they could have been the supports for the timber framework of the gallery floor.

The **inside** of the building is laid out as a small church, some 28 metres long by 20 wide. It is divided into five aisles, with octagonal pillars supporting beautiful horse-shoe arches. These pillars are crowned by fine stucco capitals, the only ones of their kind.

The history of this building can be divided into three distinct phases:

Phase one covers its construction during the middle years of the XIII century. Its irregular ground plan is only explicable by its having used the foundations of an earlier building. Only the south wall follows a symmetrical axis. For the first time in Toledo octagonal brick pillars were used, instead of the columns usually taken from some demolished building.

During the second phase, an ingenious artist influenced by the style of Granada decorated the aisles, embellished the pillars with capitals and added the medallions with their complex geometrical knotted designs. The third phase saw the changes made during the times of Cardinal Siliceo during the mid XVI century. Then the wall where the rolls had been kept was transformed into the high altar, the doorway currently in use was added, and at the head of the building the scalloped domes were added for two new altars.

The edges of the friezes around the nave were sure to have been covered in inscriptions erased, as was the polychrome work, when the building was reconsecrated as a church.

Although the **capitals** are plasterwork, they are decorated by sculpting with a gouge rather than moulded. This can be seen from the fact that even though the same themes are repeated on different capitals, slight differences can be found between them.

The **medallions** above the columns show a richness of outstandingly beautiful intricate geometrical designs.

The synagogue was reconsecrated for Christian worship around the year 1405. Like many other singular buildings, it has been used for a wide variety of purposes, including those of church worship, barracks and as a warehouse.

The miracle is that it has survived so many troubles down to the present day.

## THE SYNAGOGUE OF SAMUEL LEVY (ALSO KNOWN AS THE TRANSITO)

Once the expulsion of the Jews had taken place, the beautiful synagogue of R. Samuel Ha - Levy passed into Christian hands. Here, the inscriptions were fortunately respected, and today are not only the finest group to survive from the whole middle ages, but also supply invaluable data for placing the building in its correct historical context.

The main painting in the retable while the building was being used as a church was by Correa de Vivar. As it showed the Assumption or Transit of the Virgin, the building came to be known by the hybrid name of the "Synagoga del Transito".

The inscriptions tell us that the synagogue was inaugurated during the month of TISRI, at the close of the Seder holidays in the year of the Jewish calendar 5,117, i.e., in 1357 AD.

Two inscriptions on the outer walls were still legible during the XVIII century. One said: "This is the door of Jehovah, through which the just enter". The other was higher, next to the bell - cote, and read: "Open the doors, that a just people may enter, guardians of loyalty".

As is usual, nothing about the outside of the building gives any sign of the ornamental richness awaiting inside.

The large nave is 23 metres long by 9.5 wide, and is covered by a hand-carved ceiling of larch wood, one of the finest in Spain.

The east wall is sumptuously decorated. In the centre of this wall there is a niche (Hekal) where an ark or cupboard (Arón) could be placed to keep the Sacred Rolls (Sepharim) containing the Law (Torah). On either side of this niche there are inscriptions praising R. Samuel Ha - Levy - "A man raised to the highest, may his God go with him and extol him! He has found grace and mercy under the wings of the mighty great-winged eagle, warrior valiant above all others, the great Monarch our lord and master, our King Don Pedro".

In the floor in front of the Hekal there is a remnant of the old floor of glazed tiles.

The Toledan craftsmen decorated all four walls with two bands, one above the other. The upper band combines blind windows with others open to the light, which was filtered by beautiful lattices. The lower band has the shields of Castile and León, intertwining with a border of Arabic lettering and floral themes. This is one of the most innovative examples of Toledan Gothic - Mudejar style, which although it has a clearly Christian inspiration, is realistic beyond the limitations of a purely Gothic style, expressing an Oriental accent and rhythm.

All of these details are framed by the Psalms of David, which are inscribed in beautifully executed Hebrew characters parallel to the decorative bands around the walls.

In the south wall there are large windows which open onto the Ladies' gallery. The decoration of this was very much deteriorated, although it was restored in 1988, and now rivals that of the Oratory.

# THE SEPHARDIC MUSEUM

This is located in rooms next to the nave of the synagogue. The few remaining testimonials of Hebrew culture in Toledo have been brought together here, together with others from all over Spain.

The large granite tombstones are of outstanding archeological value. Several correspond to victims of the black plague in 1348 - 9, who were buried in the old cemetery of Toledo.

The carved beam dated 1180 is perhaps the oldest remnant of a long vanished synagogue.

There is a capital inscribed in Hebrew and Arabic, which says: "blessed be you on your entrance and on your leaving".

The bowl from Tarragona is inscribed in three different languages, and dates from the VI century. It is decorated with Hebrew and Christian symbols.

The display cabinets contain utensils and objects used in rituals associated with different holy days. A magnificent roll of the TORAH stands out, together with lamps used during the Hanukkah, trays and cups of the Pesah and bridal robes from the Sephardies of the Magreb.

# THE HOUSE AND MUSEUM OF EL GRECO

It is known from documents that El Greco lived in the abandoned palace belonging to the Marquis de Villena, Duke of Escalona, which stood on the site of what is now the Transito Park and its adjacent houses.

The building now fancifully known as the House of El Greco was in fact the palace of Samuel Levi, King Don Pedro's treasurer. It later passed into the hands of the "old" Duchess, Doña Aldonza de Mendoza, Duchess of Arjona.

*SOROLLA: portrait of the Marquis de la Vega-Inclán*

During the early years of the 20th century the Marquis de la Vega - Inclan converted the old palace into a museum to hold El Greco's paintings. In doing this he created a replica of what the painter's mansion could have been like, using furniture from the time of El Greco to create a suitable atmosphere.

There is an attractive **patio** with a tiled baseboard. From here, the dining room and a small sewing room for Doña Jerónima can be entered. She was the painter's companion and mother of his child.

The picturesque **kitchen** gives onto the large garden, under which are the vaults where Samuel Levi kept his treasure.

The studio is on the **upper floor**. This contains an extraordinary version of the "Tears of Saint Peter", together with several everyday objects, just as if they were ready for El Greco to use.

One picture stands out from those which are merely exhibited to make up numbers. This is the "View and Plan of Toledo", dating from El Greco's last period (1604 - 1614).

The virgin is descending surrounded by angels over a strange Toledan country estate. A boy holds a map which is minutely detailed and annotated. This document is essential for understanding the theories of El Greco, due to which he altered the actual positions of buildings in his pictures.

There are also paintings of all the apostles, together with a few sketches. In a downstairs room there is the hallucinatory picture of Saint Bernadino. Here El Greco elongated the body of the saint in an attempt to express spirituality. The mitres symbolize the three bishoprics which the saint renounced: Sena, Terrasa and Urbino.

*The entrance hall of the house*

## <u>THE KITCHEN</u>

The lower floor of the house ends with this room, which like the others opens onto the patio, with a view onto the porch, over the upper garden. It has the air of a normal kitchen, with a fire and chimney, benches placed next to the wall, low three - legged stools and all the implements which one would expect for a homely kitchen, fire irons and warming pans. The furnishings of this room are completed by a good collection of items of pottery, cupboards, cabinets, low tables and chairs, etc. The cabinets set into the wall are especially charming: one has a cross in relief over its doors, which may mean that it originally came from a convent. The other has a lattice set into both doors, allowing one to see inside. It is possible to make out plates and jugs, and although they are not clearly visible, this is part of the charm of cabinets of this type.

A bowl decorated in the characteristic style of Talavera and Puente del Arzobispo stands out amongst the pottery items. It shows winged animals in Eastern style.

*Altar piece of St. Bernard*

*View and plan of Toledo (El Greco)*

32    *The Tears of St. Peter*

*Cathedral*

# THE CATHEDRAL; HISTORY

The power of the Almohad factions of the Arabs in Spain was definitively restricted by the Battle of Navas de Tolosa (1212) known as "the Unfortunate" in Arab chronicles.

Toledo was no longer a frontier city, ceasing to be vulnerable to Arab attack.

Alfonso VIII and his councillor and aid Archbishop Ximénez de Rada did consider building a cathedral to commemorate the victory. The archbishop was "a learned and eminent man", who spoke several languages and had studied at the Universities of Paris and Bologna. However, the king died two years later.

Although in Leon and Burgos the cathedrals were being readied for their roofs, the Primal See in Toledo was still using the old mosque, which had been reconsecrated as the Main Church in 1086 by Alfonso VI. However, work here was started in 1221. In 1222 Pope Honorio III devoted a Bull to obtaining resources "as such a great work cannot be finished without great expense...". The first stone was ceremoniously laid in 1226, when work was already well under way.

Virtually nothing is known of the architect of the cathedral. Documents do mention a Master Builder Martin in 1227, and there is also a famous tombstone which reads: "Petras Petri magister eclesia... qui preseus templus construxit". It is not known where either of these men came from.

Even if Master Martin was not French, it is clear that he must have had in - depth knowledge of the plans and techniques used in French cathedrals, especially that at Le Mans. This is the case even though in Toledo the methods used are of unprecedented originality, especially in the ambulatory and flying buttresses at the head of the church.

The triforium gallery shows marked Toledo Mudejar influence, which may mean that it was built by Pedro Pérez (Petrus Petri) who continued the work of Master Martin. It is clearly of local inspiration, the work of an architect from the area of Toledo.

## THE WEST FRONT

As in other Gothic cathedrals, it was planned to give the main facade two symmetrical towers. However, in Toledo only the bell - tower was completed. It is 92 metres high, and contains the bell known as the "Gorda" ('The Big One'), which weighs almost 18,000 kilograms.

The other tower terminates in a lower octagonal dome. This was built by Jorge Manuel, the son of El Greco.

The towers are on either side of the facade with its three doors.

The **Pardon Door** is in the centre. It gets its name from the indulgences which were granted to those who passed through this door. The Judgement Door **on the right** is so named due to the subject shown on its tympanum, although it is also known as the Door of the Notaries. **The left - hand** door is known as both the Hell Door and the Palm Door.

The west front was restored so thoroughly in the XVIII century using granite that it lost much of its original character.

Only the three doors were left as they were. The tympanum of the central door shows the Elevation. In the central column, Christ appears in his majesty presiding over the assembled apostles: although documents mention that this was begun in 1418, both style and craftwork correspond to the time of the doors themselves, which are dated 1337.

## THE PUERTA LLANA ("FLAT DOOR")

This gets its name from the fact that it has no steps, thereby making it easier for processions to pass through, especially the procession of Corpus Christi with the float on which the Monstrance is mounted. This door used to be called "The Wagon door", as it was through here that the stone was brought in while construction was in progress.

The Ionic style of this door clashes with that of the rest of the Cathedral. It was added in 1800, under the direction of Ignacio Haan, the architect.

## LA PUERTA DE LOS LEONES ("THE DOOR OF THE LIONS")

A group of Flemish sculptors arrived in Castille in the middle years of the XV Century. Their leader was Hanequin of Brussels. He came with his brothers, Anton and Egas Cueman, together with Pedro Guas, the father of Juan, who would go on to become the architect of San Juan de los Reyes.

These men introduced the Flemish style to Toledo. Once established in Toledo, they set up a workshop with Toledan artists. This became a centre for the spread of the new forms, and from here came the master artists who were destined to raise the artistic standard of Toledo so high within the country as a whole.

In 1452 the first stone was laid for the Door of Joy, in homage to the Assumption. When the railings were added to this door in 1646, it came to be known as the "Door of the Lions" because of the figures holding the shields on the columns.

The group of foreign artists, together with many Toledan stone masons, all under the order of Hanequin, the most important master artist of the Cathedral, worked on filling the three sections of the arch around the door with angelic musicians and seraphim. Juan Alemán and Egas Cueman sculpted the statues of the apostles and Marias inside the small atrium.

Only the Virgin above the porch is not the original figure, as it was replaced in the XVIII century with one by Salvatierra.

In the spaces of the two lintels the Transit of the Virgin is shown, according to the text of the Apocryphal gospels, especially that of the Pseudo Joseph of Arimathea.

The meeting of the Apostles in the bedroom, where the Virgin lies in her coffin, is shown on the right. The scene on the left shows the coffin being taken to the Valley of Josaphat. They were attacked by the Jew, Ruben, while on their way, and his dried hands remained stuck to the coffin.

Although Saint Thomas was unable to attend, he watched the Assumption from the Mount of Olives, and the Lady rewarded him by presenting him with her girdle, shown on the small canopy of the Virgin in the division between the doors.

*The Door of the Lions*

## THE AISLES

The floor area of the cathedral makes it one of the largest in the Christian world. It is 120 metres long by 50 metres wide, and is 33 metres high in the central aisle.

The cathedral is laid out in 5 aisles (with double side aisles). This is a similar floor plan to those at Paris and Bourges, and means that the transept is incorporated into the main body of the church, and is not visible from the outside.

There were a series of attempts at solving the problem of the vaulting of the ambulatory, and the ingenious architect arrived at an original and definitive solution in Toledo. The vaults were set out in a rectangular pattern, and were triangular instead of trapezoid in shape. This was achieved by using double pillars in the exterior aisles.

The stone framework of this marvel was finished in 1493, during the time of Cardinal Mendoza.

His successors, great prelates and patrons of the arts, were able to use their immense wealth to enrich and decorate the bare stone with chapels, jewels, organs, screens, manuscripts and sculptures. It became one of the most opulent cathedrals in the Christian world.

This process was interrupted by the baroque period, which culminated in the construction of the Transparente in 1732.

It is useless to try to avoid cliches in describing Toledo cathedral. In spite of all the robberies and sackings which it has suffered, there can be few places containing so much richness, history and magnificence.

*Central aisle*

## THE DOOR OF THE LIONS (INTERIOR)

The inside of the Lion Door was transformed in the mid XVI century. Part of Hanequin's work in 1460 was respected, while in perfect harmony with this, the upper part or second wing was successfully added, in the purest Renaissance style.

The doors themselves, with their splendid walnut panels carved by Miguel Copín (son of Diego) and Diego Velasco y Anas, were put into position in 1541.

The inside of the doors are covered with bronze sheets, engraved with amazing skill by Villalpando. The handles of the doors deserve special mention for their refined taste.

Only the niche on the left hand side is occupied, by the elegant mausoleum of the generous canon Don Alonso de Rojas (d. 1577). He was the nephew of Don Francisco, ambassador of the Catholic Kings. The niche on the other side is empty. It was designed for the unfortunate Archbishop Carranza de Miranda, who died in Rome.

The sculpture of the resurrect man in the division between the doors, and the interesting representation of the Tree of Jesse in the tympanum both date from the time of Hanequin (1460).

The symbolic tree of Jesse (the genealogy of the Virgin) does not grow from King David's father's rib, but from his ear.

This is the creation of the Verb, of the Word, which enters through the ears and engenders the idea. As always, the finishing touch is the Virgin and Child.

Above this is a medallion showing the coronation of the Virgin. This is by Gregorio of Burgundy, the son of Felipe. In the side niches there are the figures of David and Solomon, carved by Miguel Copín.

This exceptional facade is crowned by the organ of the Emperor, also known as the Procession organ. This was built by Master organ builder Gonzalo de Cordoba, and was finished by Juan Gaytán, a Toledan, from 1543 - 49.

Although it is now electrified, the old system of supplying air to the organ has been preserved. This consists of two large bellows under each end of a catwalk on a rocker, such that a man had to walk constantly back and forth along the catwalk to pump the air.

## THE "TRANSPARENTE"

Several attempts were made at enlarging and illuminating the small room behind the Custody of the High Altar containing the tabernacle where the Holy Vessels are kept.

Cardinal Don Diego of Astorga, who is buried at the foot of the altar, eventually placed Narciso Tomé, a follower of Churriguera, in charge of the works. He worked on the Transparente for eleven years, from 1721 to 1732, helped by his sons. He was architect, painter and sculptor while work was under way.

*The door of the Laions (interior)*

42  *The transparente*

This baroque fantasy of Tomé, who was very much a man of his time, involved the raising of an enormous concave retable made of marble and bronze, known as "the terror of Academics, marvel of the people, always the subject of argument, and always admirable".

The centre of the altar holds the small window which lets light through into the sanctuary. Amongst the shining gold leaf are the four archangels Raphael, Gabriel, Michael and Uriel, with their respective symbols around the windows.

The altar itself is made of grey marble. In spite of the vertical, artificial nature of the perspective the scene it of the Last Supper which it depicts is well portrayed. It is crowned by three statues of the Theological Virtues. Tomé worked marble as if it were putty, combining fanciful columns with friezes of angels, and using strangely curved mouldings, embossing and statues, all in one dreamlike work.

A source of light was needed if all this fantasy were to be visible, so with cold audacity he pierced the dome above. He decorated the resulting window with paintings and sculptures to amazing effect.

No other work of art has given rise to so much bitter argument. But no matter what can be said of it, the transparente window is a colourful, dynamic and bright spectacle in the stillness and indistinct half-light of the cathedral.

## THE SACRISTY AND OTHER AUXILIARY ROOMS

Most of the cathedral museums are in the large room of the Sacristy, the Reliquary (an eight - sided room), and the Vestry which leads through to the New Museums.

The vaulted ceiling of the **large Sacristy** is decorated by the Neapolitan artist Luca Giordano (Luca fa presto). It shows the elevation of Saint Idelfonso. The 250 square metres of the ceiling are crowded by brightly coloured people and angels, all within a finely achieved perspective in the painter's unmistakable and effortless style.

*The Sacristy ceiling*

The marble altar was placed here in the XVIII Century. El Greco's **first master-piece, the Spoliation** (1579) hangs above the altar. It was one of the first paintings by the artist in Toledo.

The tunic in this painting is like a red flame, broken by the delicately painted hand. The noble, august head of Christ stands out amongst the sinister faces.

On **the right of the great** painting of the Spoliation are the crown, sword and spurs of Sancho IV, together with the dramatic painting "The Kiss of Judas", one of the few pictures with a religious subject by the great Goya.

On **the left - hand** side of El Greco's painting, the image of Our Lady of Toledo stands out. It is silver plated, and dates from the XII century. The small boxes are in enamel work from Limoges, and the reliquary in embossed silver containing the arm of Saint Eugene was presented by Saint Luis in the XIII century.

Among the many valuable paintings in this unique exhibition, the collection of the Apostles stands out. The apostles were painted by El Greco several times, although this set is remarkable for its audacity. Here the apostles are shown in flowing, strangely coloured robes. Their expressions are exalted, and El Greco painted some of their faces asymmetrically in his attempt to express the deepest thoughts of those who had been chosen.

The sculpture of Saint Francis of Assisi by Pedro de Mena deserves especial mention, as does the Great Processional Cross in the opposite cabinet. This was presented by Alfonso V of Portugal to Archbishop Don Alonso Carrillo.

A door on the left gives access to the octagonal room of the Reliquary. This is located behind the Chapel of the Virgin of Sanctuary. The eight sides of this room are walled in red and black marble, decorated with frescoes by Maella (1778).

Many relics in their reliquaries of precious metal are displayed in the niches around the walls. The room is a small museum of embossed, enamelled and shaped metal work.

It contains the "Four Quarters of the Earth", composed of enormous silver spheres made in the XVII century, engraved with maps and the symbols of the continents, and decorated with precious stones.

The small vestry is next to the Sacristy. It is full of interesting pictures, and the ceiling was painted by Claudio Coello and Jose Donoso in 1691. It shows the coat of arms of Don Pascual of Aragón, the great patron of the arts who donated his large collection of paintings for exhibition in the Sacristy.

The vestry leads through to the **Room of Ornaments and Robes.** This contains the standard of the Benionerines, which was captured in the Battle of the River Salado, 1340.

The XIV century English mitre, which belonged to Cardinal Albornoz, stands out in the great collection of rain capes, ecclesiastical robes and mitres of the Toledan Cardinals. There is also a chasuble with the shields of Castile and Aragón, which has been attributed to infant Archbishop Don Sancho of Aragón, although the heraldic devices would seem to indicate that it was the property of King Don Fernando of Antequera.

The entrance to the "New Museums" is located at the far end of this exhibition. The three floors which they occupy used to be known as "The Treasury". However, a description of these "New Museums" would overstep the limits of this compact guide.

*The Sacristy*

*The Spoliation (El Greco)*

# THE CHANCEL

The transformation of the chancel was undertaken by Cardinal Cisneros. The retable used to stand between the column of the Shepherd of Las Navas and that of the Alfaquí, just where the steps end. Behind the retable was the Chapel of the Holy Cross, which had been founded by Sancho IV as a royal pantheon.

On raising the floor for the High Altar, a crypt was created underneath. This contains the mummified body of Saint Ursula, and a group of sculptures on the same subject by Diego Copín de Holanda was also placed there. It is therefore known as the Holy Sepulchre.

To crown the prodigious **High Retable**, a great many wood carvers and their teams were employed under the directorship of Petit - Jean. The fifteen large groups of sculptures, without counting the base, are in larch wood. Rodrigo Alemán, Sebastian Almonacid, Bigarny and Copín were among those who worked on this, while two other specialists, Juan Borgoña and Francisco de Ambares, covered the finished work in gold leaf which was then coloured.

The resulting retable is a whole world of fretwork canopies, pinnacles and filigree. It took six years to complete, from 1498 to 1504. The central section begins at the lowest level of the screen above the High Altar. This is a XIV century statue of Saint Mary, covered in silver plate, and came from the earlier retable. Above this is the enormous monstrance, which inspired Enrique de Arfe. As the sanctuary containing the Host is directly behind this, the Transparente was constructed 200 years later to illuminate it. The retable continues upwards with representations of Christmas and the Assumption, and is crowned by a gigantic Calvary scene.

**The side panels of the retable** are decorated with graceful protruding arches. Under these lie the tombs sculpted by Copín de Holanda. On the right are those showing Sancho IV and Maria de Molina, while opposite are those with the figures of Alfonso VII and Doña Berenguela. Nevertheless, the coffins behind these figures actually hold the remains of Sancho IV (d. 1295), the Chapel's founder Alfonso VII (d. 1257), Sancho III (d. 1158) and the child of Alfonso XI, Don Pedro de Aguilar.

A first - rate although unknown artist closed off this presbytery with two fine symmetrical fretwork walls at the end of the XIV century.

The one wall still standing is perhaps one of the finest and most poetic works to survive from the Gothic period of Spanish art. This leads on the outside to the procession of the apostles, while inside the frieze shows the Toledan Archbishops. The Kings of Spain were shown on the other wall, but this was unfortunately demolished so that the Renaissance mausoleum of Cardinal Mendoza (d. 1494) could be built. Some of the statues from this wall have been preserved on the pillars inside.

*The retable of the High Altar*

*Detail of the retable of the High Altar*

*Detail of the retable of the High Altar*

*DETAILS OF WINDOWS*

## THE INSIDE OF THE CHOIR

The choir is entered through the grille, which is by **Master Domingo de Cespedes.** This Toledan ironworker was helped by his son - in - law Hernán Bravo in this great enterprise, the making of which lasted from 1541 to 1548. It is contemporary with the high altar, which is the work of Villalpando.

Master Domingo contracted to make this grille for 6,000 ducats. However, the work lasted for longer than he had thought, the difficulties he encountered were enormous, and so to finish it he not only had to sell all his possessions but also to borrow money.

His anguished pleas for the amount to be paid for the grille to be increased were in vain:

"I have spent all that I earned in my youth on this grille, together with a large sum of maravedies, as I have pawned everything", he wrote to Cardinal Siliceo in 1559. He did receive some help in his poverty, but the great artist died, an example of honesty and integrity, utterly ruined.

The stalls in the **lower choir** are the first work in Spain of Rodrigo Alemán, and took him six years, from 1489 to 1495.

The fifty four backs of these stalls are in carefully selected walnut wood. Rodrigo carved these with a historian's eye to show the battles and attacks, fighting and surren-

ders which had taken place during the memorable time of the conquest of Granada. It is said that during these battles, there were as many heroes as there were captains, and as many brave men as there were soldiers.

These stalls are of immense historical value. The main characters are recognizable, as are the fire arms, military tactics, ways of horse riding and forms of clothing etc. shown.

The artist gave free reign to his imagination when carving the designs on the armrests, corners, handrails and decorated brackets of the tip - up seats or "misericords". These contain chimerical animals and burlesque scenes from fables and sayings, in which the artist did not shrink from picturing erotic or even obscene details.

Cardinal Tavera decided to renovate the **upper choir** in 1535. The old one was removed and two first - rate artists were given the job of creating the new one.

**The left - hand side** (facing the altar) was assigned to Felipe de Bigaruy. He was from Burgundy, while the right - hand side is the work of Alonso de Berruguete, a temperamental and emotional artist from Palencia.

Behind the graceful porphyry column, under the series of arches designed by Covarrubias, are the famous walnut panels, the most famous Spanish Renaissance sculpture.

They were carved by Berruguete, who was at the height of his artistic powers. They overflow with fantasy and energy, the tormented and gesticulating figures expressing all the fury of the artist's imagination. Meanwhile Bigaruy, his rival, refined and elegant without abandoning his gothic heritage, calm and classical, died while working on the Archbishop's chair in 1542. The alabaster medallion on this chair is by his brother, Gregorio Pardo, and dates from 1548.

Above the **Archbishop's chair** Berruguete crowned the achievement of the finest and most glorious choir in the world by sculpting the Transfiguration on Mount Tabor, in a single gigantic alabaster block.

The delicate series of arches is complemented by an **alabaster frieze.** This was made by the above-mentioned artists and their assistants, and shows a concise version of the genealogy of Christ, according to the gospels of Saint Luke and Saint Matthew.

Within this unique choir, the "Prime" (high) **Altar** is framed by graceful balusters carved by Rui Díaz del Corral in 1564. The "White Virgin" in marble is French, from the XIV century. Her smiling face and radiant maternal happiness answer the touch of her child.

In the centre is the great lectern. The base of this is in the form of a battlemented castle, with figures of the apostles which were brought

*The White Virgin*

from Germany in 1425. The great eagle was added in 1646. Its wings are outspread to take the weight of the heavy parchment books used by the choir.

# THE CATHEDRAL TREASURY

Until it was moved by Fonseca to its current location, the three vaults in front of the Treasury formed the Chapel of the New Kings. It was here that the Kings of the Trastámara dynasty were buried. The area under the bell tower, where the Treasury is kept today, served as the Sacristy.

The **Main Cathedral Treasury.** The beautiful facade is by Alonso de Covarrubias, and is crowned by a niche containing the "Quo Vadis" group of figures, with the coat of arms of Archbishop Tavera and worker Canon López de Ayala. As well as being known as the "Quo Vadis", this chapel has also been called that of "Saint John" or "The Tower".

The work is Mozarab in style (the stalactites) and is unique in Toledo as it is in wood. It dates from the Trastámara dynasty, and the following display cabinets deserve especial mention:

The **first cabinet on the right**: this contains a pectoral cross and ring of burnt topazes and diamonds, which belonged to Cardinal Goma. There is also a beautiful cross which was presented by Pope John XXIII, and a chest for the Virgin's crown.

In the **second display cabinet** on the

right a fine three - volume parchment annotated bible stands out. It belonged to Saint Luis, and contains more than 3,000 illustrations.

There is also an engraved silver tray decorated by outstanding work in high relief. This has been attributed to Cellini, although it does bear the stamp: "Matias Melinc. Belgia".

The **Central display cabinet**. This holds the Processional Monstrance for the Consecrated Bread. Standing on an XVIII century pedestal, and supported by four silver plated angels, it is one of the most ostentatious works in precious metals of the Christian world. It was made of silver by the German artist Enrique de Arfe during the early years of the XVI century.

The inner monstrance is made entirely of gold, precious stones and enamel work. It came from the estate of The Catholic Queen, Isabel, and was made by an unknown goldsmith. Tradition has it that the first gold brought from America was used in its making.

Its delicate columns enamelled with floral motifs hold the pyx itself, where the consecrated bread is placed.

Enrique de Arfe created this wonderful jewel in the form of a gothic tower during the years 1516 - 1524. It was gold plated at the end of the XVI century.

This monstrance is paraded every year through the streets of Toledo on a special platform, designed to keep it upright over all the slopes and hills of the city.

The **small display cabinet on the left** holds the imperial crown of the Patron Saint of Toledo. This used to be Queen Isabel's royal crown, but in 1586 the Toledan jeweller Aloejo de Montoya added the shell, giving it an imperial style. The historical interest of the object itself is heightened by the intrinsic value of the precious stones which it contains. The outstanding emerald in the diamond cross is especially valuable.

The wealth contained in this Treasury is too great to be described in a book of this size.

Up to 64 exhibits are missing. These include the richly decorated mantle of the Virgin of the Sanctuary, which held 80,000 pearls. All of these vanished in 1936.

*The Monstrance*

*Santo Tomé Street*

# THE BURIAL OF THE COUNT OF ORGAZ

The burial chapel of Don Gonzalo Ruíz de Toledo, gentleman of Orgaz and Head Notary of Castile, lies at the foot of the church of Santo Tomé. This Toledan nobleman died in 1323 at the end of a pious life, during which he made generous donations to religious institutions.

The legend surrounding his burial had been passed down from generation to generation since his death. According to this legend, those at his funeral were amazed when Saint Augustine and Saint Steven came down from heaven, took up the body and laid it in his tomb. They clearly heard the words: "Such is the reward for those who serve God and his Saints".

The gentleman of Orgaz (who unlike his descendants never had the title of Count) had bequeathed both money and goods in his will to help the priest and poor of the parish of Santo Tomé, to be paid annually by the inhabitants of the town of Orgaz.

Over the years, the people of Orgaz began to avoid making the payments stipulated in the will, and the parish priest took them to court. He won his case, and wanted to commemorate this by placing a painting of the legendary events at the funeral over the tomb of Don Gonzalo Ruíz.

The **picture** which El Greco painted meets the conditions laid down by the priest, even though it contains contemporary styles of dress and the faces of people alive at the time the picture was painted, making it an anachronism. The resulting work is an exceptional sign of El Greco's arrival at complete artistic maturity.

The **contract** was signed on Saint Joseph's day, 1586, and the picture was handed over by the artist at Christmas, having taken only nine months to complete.

The painting is divided into upper and lower sections by a line of gentlemen with thoughtful, concentrated expressions, more serene than sad. The levels above and below them are different in both theme and style.

The aged nobility of Saint Augustine, who is supporting the back of the body, contrasts with the youthfulness of Saint Steven, whose hand seems to be holding the legs of the apparently weightless body.

The page in the foreground holding a torch and pointing at the central scene is Jorge Manuel, son of El Greco. The signature on his handkerchief is in Greek, and is dated 1579. This does not coincide with the actual date of the painting, which was finished in 1586.

The gentleman directly above Saint Steven's head is possibly a self - portrait. He does not seem to be taking part in the burial, and looks out of the painting at those who have come to see it.

The vestments are painted with masterful technique, especially in the details of their embroidery in gold thread. They hang in stately, rigid folds, which contrast with the vibrating light in the delicate white cloth of the surplice, itself a wonderful display of technique.

The physical world ends where the Toledan nobleman are solemnly gathered. Above them, everything changes, and there are clouds, figures and angels painted in an elongated style in arbitrary colours.

*The burial of the count of Orgaz*

Above the group of noblemen there is a blond angel in the centre of a cloudburst. The robes of this angel are being blown upwards by an invisible wind, and the angel is holding a chrysalis. The chrysalis has the form of a new born child, and the angel is trying to push this through the neck of the womb, thereby symbolizing re-birth in God the Father.

The soul abandons its physical remains on the earth, rising up into a perfect triangulation of Christ the Judge, his clothes irradiating luminous white light, and below Him the Virgin on the left and John the Baptist on the right. The two lower figures are intervening on behalf of the arriving soul, and while the Virgin wears flowing blue and carmine robes, John the Baptist has only a sheepskin to cover the nakedness of his disproportionate body.

This painting is a peak of human achievement, and is the artistic heritage of mankind as a whole. It combines technical mastery with a sure hand, inspiration and artistic talent with poetic fantasy and imagination.

## ALCANTARA BRIDGE

The River Tagus reaches Toledo after winding through fertile market gardens. At the city it narrows between two granite hills, to follow its course around the rock on which the city is built.

The Al - Qantara bridge lies astride the river just at the point where this narrows. In spite of its Arab name (Al - Qantara means "The bridge") it has Roman origins. This can be seen from the many stone slabs incorporated in its foundations and piers. It was here that the roads linking Toledo to Mérida converged with those going to Cesaraugusta (Zaragoza) via Sigüenza.

The Visigoths maintained and used this bridge. A poem by Venancio Fortunato tells of how Princess Gelesvinta, the daughter of Atanagildo, left on her journey to marry the cruel king of the Graucos, Chilperico.

Her parents foresaw her unfortunate destiny, and the wagons loaded with rich goods and the bride's dowry "stopped in the middle of the bridge" for the bitter farewell.

The bridge must have been intact when the Arabs arrived, although it was seriously damaged on several occasions while the central power of Cordoba tried to bring the rebellious city of Toledo under control.

Following a two year siege, Abd - al-Rahman III surrendered Toledo in 932. His first concern was to repair the heavily damaged bridge, which Arab chronicles say had suffered from the Toledan tendency to strive against the Caliph for self - government.

As the bridge was both the main way into the city and its most vulnerable point, the Caliph ordered it to be fortified by the construction of a fort (Al - Hizen) linking the bridge defenses (Bab al-Qantara) to the palaces and Alcázar, seat of government and barracks of the guard, to strictly control this entrance to the city.

Descriptions of this bridge by contemporary geographers and historians praise it as a technical marvel. They say that it had "only one arch", and this is thought to mean

*Alcántara bridge and the Alcázar*

that it crossed the river in a single span, the others being storm overflows. The bridge is thought to have had three arches, as this arrangement would be most pleasing aesthetically. The third arch could have been in the massive left pier itself. There is still a small opening here. It is clearly Arab in origin, and corresponds to the path along the river bank. This opening could date from the reconstruction ordered by Almanzor in the year 997, at approximately the same time as the Bab al - Mardun mosque was built.

The great flood of 1257, when it rained continuously from August to December, seriously damaged the bridge. The following year Alfonso X "The Wise" had it repaired, reinforcing the giant pier with an enormous cutwater.

One of the original towers still stands. It is on the city side, and was rebuilt in 1484, while Gómez Manrique was chief magistrate. It bears the coat of arms of the Catholic Kings. The completely enclosed fort used to stand on this side of the bridge.

In 1961 the Bab al-Qantara was restored as far as possible. However, the other two walls had been destroyed in 1864 when the road was built.

## SAN MARTIN BRIDGE

Toledo used to be supplied with granite for building, coal and other necessities from the mountains of Toledo and Extremadura. A bridge linking the city to the west was therefore needed, and would also have been useful for the passage of cattle.

Experts say that the tower downstream from the bridge, near the walls which here come close to the river, is a remnant of a pontoon bridge which was in existence from Arab times. Known as the **"Baño de la Cava",** it is associated with the local legend of the love of Don Rodrigo and Florinda.

The old bridge suffered heavy damage from the many battles which took place nearby, and flooding. The floods of 1203 finally destroyed the pontoon bridge, and the construction of a new stone bridge a short way up stream was mooted.

There are no documents showing when work on the new bridge started, and neither is the name of the ingenious architect responsible for the central arch known. However, it is known that it was finished in the early years of the XIV century.

The bridge gets its name from its proximity to the parish dedicated to saint Martin.

The structure of this bridge was severely damaged during the fratricidal battles between Don Pedro I and his stepbrother Don Enrique. Archbishop Tenorio therefore decided on complete rebuilding, and it was this decision which gave rise to one of the most appealing legends to have sprung from the city.

*St. Martin bridge and Baño de la Cava*

When the bridge was at an advanced stage of construction, the engineer responsible for the project realized that, once it had been closed and the scaffolding removed, the central arch would not be able to support the weight of the heavy carts bringing in stone for the building of the cathedral. The work of years would be wasted, together with all that the rebuilding had cost. The best that the engineer could hope for himself would be ignominy and a ruined reputation. He told no one, and became more and more depressed with each stone added to the bridge.

Eventually he confided in his wife, but still the work went on, and he could find no solution to the problem.

His wife tried to cheer him up, but one night she crept unseen out of their house, and went to the bridge where after climbing the scaffolding she set light to the thick beams supporting the arch.

Once the supports had burnt through, the unfinished arch of the bridge collapsed. This fire was thought to be due to an unfortunate accident. Work was restarted, and the engineer was able to correct his original calculations. The result is the fine arch of the bridge, spanning 40 metres, 27 metres above the river at the centre.

Legend has tried to give the engineer's resourceful wife her reward for saving her husband's honour and reputation, by saying that the sculpture inserted in the key stone of the bridge is of her face.

However, and in spite of the erosion of the stone which has taken place over the years, the mitred head of the archbishop who ordered the bridge to be restored can still be made out.

66    *San Martín bridge*

## THE ALCAZAR AND ITS MUSEUMS

Dominating the houses crowded on the Cervantine hill, "glory of Spain and light of its cities", stands the imposing bulk of the Alcázar (royal palace).

This site was doubtless used by the Romans as a praetorium (military base). The line followed by the Roman wall of "Toletum" started here, to go down to the Arco de la Sangre (the "Arch of Blood" in Zocodover). Remains can still be seen in the Calle de las Armas, on the way down to the Paseo del Miradero.

Nothing remains of Visigoth times here. Nevertheless, the door in the south west corner dates from the period of Arab domination, from the time of Abd - al - Rahman (835).

Alfonso VI rebuilt the Alcázar on the reconquest of the city. Tradition has it that the first governor was El Cid, who stationed his Castilian and Aragonese troops here.

The Toledan King Alfonso X "The Wise" caused the east wall to be built in the XIII century. The battlements of this wall and its turrets can still be seen.

In one of the underground rooms of the Alcázar, the bedroom of Doña Blanca, unfortunate wife of Don Pedro I "The Cruel" has been reproduced. This is to commemorate the days which she spent imprisoned here.

It was Carlos V who adapted and converted the building into a royal palace. For this he employed the finest architects of his day, including Covarrubias and Juan de Herrera.

Once the royal court had moved definitively to Madrid, the Alcázar was occasionally still used for royal visits. The first of the major fires which it has suffered occurred during the Wars of Succession in 1710.

A hundred years later, in 1810, Napoleon's troops set fire to the building when they left the city. It was taken over for use as an Infantry Academy in 1846.

*Partial view and the Alcázar*

It was the scene of heroic resistance during the Spanish Civil War (1936) when it was besieged. Once again, it suffered grave damage.

It was rebuilt once again, now containing a museum of the siege, and the Museum of Knives and Swords in a large room. The exhibition shows how this science has developed from stone knives to the famous blades of Toledo steel. Another exhibition holds a collection of fire - arms, from the earliest days of gunpowder down to modern automatic weapons. Yet another museum holds trophies, souvenirs and uniforms from the times when Spanish troops were in Africa. The Alcázar also houses the Romero Ortiz collection of historic objects and medals.

*The Alcázar before the fire*

# MADRID

## ...ART
## ...HISTORY

BY: JOSE JOAQUIN HORTAL DE PRIEGO
TRANSLATED BY: DAVID FRICKER

# THE STORY OF MADRID

There are many myths about the origins of Madrid. It is now one of the most modern cities in the centre of the Iberian Peninsula.

Although it is true that important archeological remains from the Paleolithic have been found on the banks of the Manzanares river, with many stone tools and fossils of mammoths, the first documentary historical mention of Madrid is from the times of the Arabian era. In the 9th century (the year 873) during the reign of Sultan Mohammed I (the son of Abderraman II) the Arabs constructed a fort on the hill where the Royal Palace now stands. The formed a part of the defensive lines of Tulaitola (Toledo). The Arabs called this fort Mayrit, which is an Arabic form of the latin word "matrice", meaning spring or source of water.

The Arab population lived on two hills. One was that now occupied by the Royal Palace, where the fort and main mosque stood. This hill was surrounded by a wall of flint and bricks, the remains of which may be seen in Bailén street, while in the garden in front of the palace there are the foundations of a tower. The other hill was that known as Vistillas, to the south west, where the Seminary and Basilica of St. Francisco now stand. These hills were separated by a valley and stream (now Segovia Street) and have been joined by the viaduct of Bailén Street.

Where the wall stood in the Plaza de Puerta Cerrada, next to the Plaza Mayor, there is an inscription on a wall: "I was founded on springs of water, my walls are of fire (flint)".

The Arab city was small, with no more than 1,500 inhabitants, and contained Jewish and Mozarab communities.

The city was conquered by Alfonso VI in 1083 in his advance towards Toledo. From the 12th to the 14th centuries Madrid was a small city within the reign of Castilla y Leon, where Jews, Mudejars (subject Arabs) and Christians lived together. The first municipal charter of Madrid dates from the year 1200. In 1309 Ferdinand IV summoned the Court or Parliament, and the kings of the Trastámara dynasty Henry III, Juan II and Henry IV used the city as an occasional residence, due to the abundance of game. The shield of Madrid shows a bear and a strawberry tree, as the city was surrounded by large forests with many bears and big game.

The first Arab palace was enlarged by the kings of Castilla and those of the Austrian dynasty. Charles I used it several times, and granted the city the title of Imperial and Crowned.

In 1561, Philip II (the son of Charles I) decided to move the court and administration to Madrid from Toledo. He may have done this as Madrid was closer to El Escorial, where he projected the construction of the San Lorenzo monastery, in which he died and is buried. Madrid at this time had no more than 15,000 inhabitants, and was to remain the capital of Spain, except for the years 1601 - 1606, during which Philip III took the court to Valladolid. During the Austrian dynasty churches, monasteries and convents were built, together with the Plaza Mayor and the Palacio del Buen Retiro, etc. Miguel de Cervantes died in the city in 1616, and during the 17th century the painter Velázquez lived and worked here, as did the writers Quevedo, Góngora, Lope de Vega and Calderón de la Barca.

The capital city of Madrid grew by more than 40,000 inhabitants in 100 years, and on the initiative of the Bourbon kings became a great city in architectural terms from 1710 onwards. Philip V, the grandson of Luis XIV, ordered the fabulous Royal Palace to be built on the site of the old palace of the Austrian dynasty, which had been destroyed in a fire in 1734. The Mayor, the Marquis de Vadillo, constructed great Avenues together with the baroque architect Pedro de Ribera, such as the Virgen del Puerto, together with Toledo bridge and the Hospice, fountains and the church and barracks of Conde Duque.

The son of Philip V, Charles III "The Mayor King" ordered great neo-classical architects such as Sabatini, Ventura Rodríguez and Marquet to bring Madrid to the forefront of European architecture. The finest buildings of the city date from this time: the Prado Concourse, with the fountains of Neptune, Apollo and Cybele, the botanical gardens, the astronomical observatory, the Natural History Collection (now the Prado Museum), academies, the sewer system, lighting, Alcalá Gate, Retiro Park and San Carlos Hospital. Nevertheless, as Madrid was an administrative city it lacked a strong economic infrastructure, and the population did not increase by very much during this time.

In the 19th century, which began with the disastrous War of Independence, Madrid underwent several reforms in city planning. Under José I Bonaparte many new squares were constructed, as Madrid at this time still had a partially medieval street plan. During the reign of Ferdinand VII, and especially that of his daughter Isabela II, palaces, gardens, fountains, walks, parks and Toledo Arch were built.

The Marquis of Salamanca, Minister during the reign of Isabela II, built Recoletas Avenue and the quarter of the city which bears his name. The first part of the Castellana Avenue also dates from this time, as do the middle class quarters of Chamberi and Argüelles. These quarters are laid out in the form of a grid, and they contain tall buildings with gates for carriages, beautiful balconies and bay windows.

During the reign of Alfonso XII several beautiful buildings were constructed. These include the Bank of Spain, Linares Palace and the Post Office Building in Cybele Square and the Ministry of Agriculture. Work on building Almudena Cathedral started at this time, together with Atocha Basilica. Some of these buildings were finished during the first decades of the 20th century.

Alfonso XIII ordered the building of the Gran Via in 1910. He also inaugurated the first underground line in the city, from Sol to Cuatro Caminos, and the Hospital de Jornaleros in Maudes Street. Most importantly of all, he opened the Great City of the University to the North of the city, in 1927.

The Civil War from 1936 - 1939 was enormously damaging for the city, and during the rule of General Francisco Franco (1940 -1975) it became an important industrial centre and grew very rapidly. The population rose from 1,000,000 inhabitants in 1945 to more than 3,800,000 during this time, and many new quarters for workers were constructed. The Moncloa and España Squares, amongst others, date from this time, as does part of Castellana Avenue and the Nuevos Ministerios.

With the coming into being of the democratic constitutional monarchy in 1975, part of Madrid was constructed in the form of a futuristic city: the northern end of Castellana Avenue (the AZCA complex) was built, together with gardens. Urban infrastructure was put into place, as this had been lacking due to the rushed construction of much of the city. Mr. Enrique Tierno Galván, Mayor from 1979 to 1986, worked enormously hard to give Madrid a cleaner future, and to recover the traditions of the city.

The population of Madrid has declined over recent years. This is partially due to a decline in the birth rate, and also to the fact that many of the inhabitants have moved out to new residential areas outside the city. Its population is currently approximately 3,000,000 people.

Madrid is located virtually at the centre of the Iberian Peninsula, on a series of small hills at the banks of the Manzanares River. The average height of the city is 650 m. above sea level.

The climate of Madrid is continental and dry. Winters are cold, and the temperature falls below zero on some nights. Summers are hot, and temperatures may rise above 40° C. The Spring and Autumn are especially pleasant times of year.

*Gasparini Room, Royal Palace*

*Armoury Square and main facade of the Royal Palace*

## THE ROYAL PALACE (on Bailen Street)

This was built on the site of the Arab fortress which formed the origins of the city, and which later became the Royal Palace of the Austrian dynasty. It was destroyed by a fire on Christmas night, 1734. Philip V, the French grandson of Luis XIV and the first king of the Bourbon dynasty, came to power after the death of Charles II and a long war of succession against Archduke Charles of Austria. He wished to have a grand palace in Madrid, like the one at Versailles which his grandfather had built. The wife of Philip V, the Italian Isabel Farnese, who was a great art-lover, advised him to call in the Italian architect Filippo Juvarra in 1735. When Juvarra died, it was another Italian, Giovanni Battista Sacchetti, who drew up the definitive project in Italian Baroque style. He used a square design with a central patio, with granite from the Guadarrama mountains and limestone from Colmenar.

Work started in 1738, and was not finished until 1764, during the reign of

*West Facade and Campo del Moro*

78

Charles III, who was the first monarch to live there. It took many more years for the interior decoration to be completed.

As it was constructed on a hill by the River Manzanares, the foundations of the building consist of enormous walls and stepped platforms with vaulted interiors, which reach down almost to the river on the West side. The garden of Campo del Moro is on this side. It was designed in the 19th century with woods, paths and fountains, such as those of the Tritons and the Shells. This garden also holds the Museum of Carriages, which holds a collection of coaches, berlin carriages, landaus and carriages belonging to the kings of Spain since the 16th century, as well as saddles and tapestries.

The high Sabatini gardens are on the North side, next to Bailén Street. These gardens were created when the stables were removed, in 1933.

The main entrance is in the South facade. It is also known as the Armoury Square, and changes of the guard are held here on the first Wednesday of each month. Receptions using antiques carriages also take place here, when ambassadors are presenting their Credentials.

The interior decoration of the Palace makes it one of the most beautiful in Europe. It contains magnificent frescos by Italian artists such as Corrado Giaquinto and Giovanni Battista Tiéplo, Anton Rafael Mengs the German, and Spanish artists such as Francisco Bayeu, Mariano Salvador Maella and Vicente López. Its crystal chandeliers, Flemish tapestries, rococo, neoclassical and imperial style furniture, porcelain, clocks, portraits and paintings all go toward making the Palace the finest museum in the city.

The stairway giving access to the Palace was designed by Sabatini. This is used to go up to visit the official chambers, of which the most outstanding are:

The **Throne Room:** this is in rococo style, and the vaulted ceiling is covered in an al fresco painting. This was painted in 1764 by Tiépolo, who was from Venice. This room contains furniture, clocks, mirrors, and red damasks on the walls with silver thread borders. There are also statues showing the cardinal virtues, together with others from the collection of the seven planets. The crystal and silver chandeliers are Venetian, and are the finest in the Palace.

*The Royal Palace, Cathedral and St. Francisco*

*Throne Room, Royal Palace*

The **Gasparini room** is a masterwork of the rococo period. It was designed in its entirety by Matias Gasparini, and is decorated with silks that are hand - embroidered with silver thread. The ceiling is decorated with stuccoes, and the same design is reflected in the furniture, mirrors and marble floor. There are bronze candelabra and a beautiful mosaic table.

The **Porcelain room** is decorated with porcelain plaques following a design by the Italian Jose Gricci, which were made in the Buen Retiro factory, Madrid. This factory was founded by Charles III, with Italian technicians from the Capodimonte workshop.

The **Ceremonial Dining Room** was inaugurated in 1879, for the wedding of Alfonso XII with his second wife, Maria Cristina of Habsburg - Lorraine. It is the most impressive room of its type in Europe, and can seat 145 diners. It is decorated with 16th century Flemish tapestries, chandeliers made of bronze and crystal, porcelain from Sevres and frescos by Mengs and Bayeu.

The **Chapel** was built by the neoclassical Spanish architect, Ventura Rodriguez. Its floor plan is in the shape of a Greek cross, and it contains magnificent frescos by Corrado Giaquinto.

The **Armoury** was founded by Philip II. It contains the most important collection of arms and armour in Spain. These items belonged to Maximilian of Austria, Philip the Beautiful, Prince Charles, Boabdil, Sebastian of Portugal and the other kings of the Austrian dynasty.

*Ceremonial Dining Room, Royal Palace*

*Philip V (detail)*

## THE PLAZA DE ORIENTE

This lies in front of the Royal Palace. Construction of this square started during the reign of José I Bonaparte (1808 - 13) with the demolition of buildings that had stood there. The Plaza was finished in the reign of Isabel II. The finest equestrian statue in Madrid stands in the centre. It shows King Philip IV on horseback, and was cast in bronze by Pietro Tacca, the Italian, following a painting by Velázquez that may be seen in the Prado. The sketch showing the bearing of the horse, which stands only on its hind legs, was made by Galileo Galilei.

The most outstanding building in this Plaza is the Royal Theatre, also known as the Opera House. It was built in 1850 during the reign of Isabel II by Antonio López Aguado. Limestone statues of the kings of the old kingdoms in the Iberian Peninsula stand around the Plaza.

*Oriente Square*

*Convent of the Incarnation*

## <u>THE CONVENT OF THE INCARNATION</u> (in the Plaza de la Encarnación)

This is in the North East of the Plaza de Oriente, and was founded by Margarita de Austria, wife of Philip III, as an enclosed convent for nuns of the order of the Recollects of St. Augustine. Gómez de Mora was the architect of this building in the style of Herrera and the baroque, which was built in the Madrid fashion, with brick walls covered in flint.

The church here was restored by Ventura Rodríguez. Its marble high altar contains a painting of the Annunciation by Vicente Carducho, together with sculptures of St. Augustine and St. Monica by a member of the school of Gregorio Fernández. The paintings on the side altars are also by Vicente Carducho, while the frescos are by Zacarías González Velázquez, a painter of the 18th century.

Inside the convent there are interesting portraits of the members of the Royal House of Hapsburg, and paintings by Cajés, Carducho, Román, Carreño, Ribera and Bartolomé González, together with sculptures by Gregorio Fernández. The cloisters are very fine, and contain altars with ceramics from Talavera. The choir is also of interest, with sculptures by Boussonet, Perronius and Caromona, and above all there is a fine Reliquary, the ceiling of which was painted by Vicente Carducho in the 17th century

## THE CONVENT OF THE ROYAL DISCALCED NUNS (Plaza de las Descalzas)

This is the finest example of a 16th century convent remaining in Madrid. It was firstly a palace belonging to the Treasurer of Charles I, Alonso Gutiérrez. It was converted into a monastery by Juana of Austria, who had been born in it, in 1557 for nuns of the Franciscan Clarisas order. These came from the convent at Gandia, from which they were brought by St. Francis of Borja, Juana's Spiritual Director. Juana was the daughter of Charles I. She was the sister of Philip II and the widow of Prince Juan Manual (son of Juan III of Portugal and Catalina of Austria, the sister of Charles I). Juana was the mother of Sebastian of Portugal, who was killed in the battle of the Alcazarquivir in Morocco.

Juana of Austria was regent of Spain when Philip II left for England to marry Mary Tudor. She died in 1573 in El Escorial, from where her body was brought to this convent for burial. Juana married when she was 17, and was widowed 11 months later.

*Convent of the Royal Discalced Nuns*

Noble and royal ladies took holy orders in this convent, bringing it large endowments. It is due to this that it still preserves important art works.

The main stairs are in renaissance style. They were decorated with frescos by Antonio de Perda and Claudio Coello in the 17th century.

The collection of tapestries showing "The Triumph of the Eucharist" are based on drawings by Rubens. This collection was a gift from Isabel Clara Eugenia, the daughter of Philip II and Governor - General of the Low Countries. It is one of the finest in the world dating from the 17th century. A Van Dyck portrait of Isabel is still kept here.

Nuns take care of several chapels in the Upper Cloisters. These contain good paintings and sculptures by Luini and Luisa Roldán, "La Roldana". Above all there is Becerra's famous "Christ lying down". A monstrance is kept in the side of this figure, in which the Sacrament is placed during the Good Friday procession.

There are several nun's cells in the Lower Cloister. The most interesting of these is the one that belonged to Sister Margarita de la Cruz, Archduchess of Austria. She was the daughter of Maximilian II and Maria of Austria (the daughter of Charles I). She lived in the Convent for 20 years, following the death of her husband.

The collection of portraits of members of the House of Austria by great painters is unique. These include Cristobal Morales, Sánchez Coello, Pantoja de la Cruz, Pourbus, Rubens, Claudio Coello and Van Aechen. There is also an exceptional collection of other paintings, that includes works by Van der Weyden, Van Eyck, Bosch, Isambrandt, Breughel, Zurbarán, Orrente and Titian, together with sculptures by Pedro de Mena, Risueño, Pereira and Gregorio Fernández.

*Almudena Cathedral*

## <u>ALMUDENA CATHEDRAL</u> (Bailén Street)

This lies in front of the Plaza of the Armoury of the Royal Palace. Our Lady of the Almudena is the patron of the Cathedral, the Arab meaning of "Almudena" being fort or military strong point. According to tradition, the Virgin appeared over one of the walls of the old Arab fortress. There is a statue of Philip II at the end of the street between the Royal Palace and the Cathedral. There is a fine view of the Manzanares valley, the Casa de Campo and the Guardarrama mountains from the nearby balcony.

As Madrid was not an episcopal see it did not have a cathedral, until on March 9th, 1884, Pope Leo XIII created the diocese of Madrid - Alcalá in his bull "Romani Pontifices".

On April 4th, 1883, Alfonso XII laid the first stone of the future cathedral, which was also to be the pantheon of his first wife, his cousin Maria de las Mercedes of Orleans and Bourbon, who had died of tuberculosis just six months after marrying him. The original neogothic project for this building was drawn up by Francisco Cubas, the marquis of Cubas. The Cathedral crypt where Maria de las Mercedes was due to be buried was consecrated in 1911, although her body still lies in El Escorial. This crypt is neo-Romanic in style and is very dark. Its chapels contain notable tombs from the 19th century. There is a fine 14th century painting on plaster showing the "Virgin of the Fleur-de-Lis" in the left transept.

The Marquis of Cubas' original project was modified in 1944 by the architects Charles Sidro and Ferdinand Chueca - Goitia, and the Cathedral was finished in 1993 and consecrated by Pope John Paul II on June 15th, 1993. The facades are in neoclassical - Herrerian style, while the dome by Chueca - Gotia is 75 m high, and is neo-baroque in style.

The interior of the Cathedral is full of light. It is neogothic in style, and is divided into three naves set out in the form of a cross, with an apse aisle. It is 99 m long and 65 m wide at the transept. It is built of sandstone, limestone from Colmenar and granite.

The high altar is of green marble from Granada. The figure of Christ crucified over the altar is a 17th century baroque work by Juan de Mesa. The painting behind the altar showing the Spoliation of Christ is from the 17th century, and is by Francisco Rizzi. The walnut wood choirstalls date from the end of the 16th century, and came from the old church of Carmen.

The side chapels are dedicated to saints and devout individuals from Madrid. Some of these chapels have yet to be decorated. The most outstanding features of these chapels include: in the first on the right there is an 18th century figure of St. John the Baptist, by Michel. The retable in the right transept was made by Juan de Borgoña in the early years of the 16th century, and the image of Our Lady of Almudena, patron saint of the city, dates from the same time. The tomb of St. Isidore is very interesting, and dates from the 13th century. It shows the painting of Christ Lying Down by Juan de Ávalos, while in the first chapel to the left there is a 17th century figure of Christ Tied to the Column, by Giaccomo Colombo.

## SAN FRANCISCO EL GRANDE (Plaza de San Francisco)

This church is dedicated to Our Lady of the Angels, and was built on the site where St. Francis of Assisi constructed a small hut next to a hermitage, while he was on pilgrimage to Santiago de Compostella. Construction of the church which stands here now was started in 1761, based on a project drawn up by the Franciscan Francisco Cabezas. This project was inspired by the Pantheon in Rome, and was continued by Sabatini. The 33 m diameter dome was finished in 1784 by Miguel Fernández, and is only surpassed in diameter by that of the above - mentioned Pantheon of Agrippa in Rome (43.4 m) and the one in St. Peters by Miguel Angel (42.34 m).

This is the most impressive 18th or 19th century church in Madrid. It contains statues by Villmitjana, Samsó, Bellver, Suñol and Benlliure. Its chapels hold paintings by Bayeu, Maella, Castillo, Ferro, Casado de Alisal, Carlos L. Ribera and Plasencia. Especial mention must be made of a fine painting by Goya in the first chapel to the left of the main entry, which is dedicated to St. Bernardino. This is a self - portrait, and it was thanks to this work that Goya was recognised at Court.

The museum is also worth a visit. It holds works by Pacheco, Carducci, Cerezo, Carnicero, Alonso Cano and Zurbarán, together with an exceptional set of choir stalls, which come from Paular Monastery.

*St. Francis the Great*

## THE GATE OF TOLEDO (Plaza Puerta de Toledo)

The architect López Aguado began construction of this gate during the reign of José I Bonaparte, in honour of Napoleon. It is located at the way out of the city leading to Toledo, the historical and religious capital of Spain. A curious fact is that this gate was finished during the reign of Ferdinand VII, to commemorate the triumph over Napoleon. It is neo-classical in style.

*Toledo Gate*

## TOLEDO BRIDGE (on Calle Toledo)

This is the most beautiful of the bridges in Madrid. It was built over the River Manzanares by the baroque architect Pedro de Ribera during the reign of Philip V, from 1720 - 1725, when the Marquis of Vadillo was Chief Magistrate of the City. This bridge was in use until quite recent times as the main way out of the city towards Toledo. It is currently a pedestrian bridge.

In the centre of the bridge there are stone statues of St. Isidore and St. Maria de la Cabeza, his wife, who are patron saints of the city.

The Vicente Calderón (or Manzanares) football stadium stands close to this bridge. It belongs to the Atlético de Madrid Club, and was built in the 1960's. It holds up to 65,000 people.

*Toledo Gate (general view)*

*Cascorro Square*

## THE RASTRO

This quarter lies close to Toledo Gate, behind the Toledo Gate market building, which was built in 1934 and used to house the central fish market. It is bounded by the Plaza de Cascorro, Embajadores Street and the Ronda de Toledo. The main street of the Rastro is Ribera de Curtidores, and it is here since the times of the Catholic Kings that a typical street market has been held. Every Sunday morning a fascinating open - air market is held here, like the Parisian flea market or Portobello in London. It is possible to find the strangest things here, while the shops are the cheapest in the city. The antique market is worth visiting.

*The Palace of the Duke of Uceda in Mayor Street*

## CALLE MAYOR

The main street of Madrid in the reign of the Austrian Dynasty, it links the Royal Palace with the main square. The *Palace of the Duke of Uceda* stands where this street joins Bailén street. He was favourite and Minister of King Philip III. Typical of the monumental architecture of the time, it was designed by the military architect, Alonso de Turrillo. The *Palace of Abrantes,* on the other side of the street, dates from the same time. Now used by the Italian Institute of Culture, it stands where the Palace of the Duchess of Éboli once was.

The *Church of St. Nicholas de los Servitas,* behind the Palace of Abrantes, has a magnificent 12th century bell - tower, the oldest Christian structure in Madrid. It is in brick Roman-Mudejar style, and is similar to those found in Toledo, as well as the Church of St. Peter the Old. It is used by Italian the community in Madrid, and Alonso de Ercilla was baptized here in 1533. Juan de Herrera, Philip II's great architect is buried here.

The *Church of the Sacrament* (1671) is next to the Palace of the Duke of Uceda. This is now a military church, and is in typical Madrid baroque style. It is cross-shaped, with a single wide nave, a flat upper end, short transept and dome. Madrid baroque used only granite for foundations and facades, while the rest of buildings were constructed of cheaper brick. It has good interior decorations and murals.

The *Church of St. Miguel* (1739 - 46) is in Sacramento Street. It is late baroque style, by Giáccomo Bonavia. It has an original convex facade, topped by two towers with spires and curved front walls. Paid for by Luis de Borbón, Cardinal of Toledo, it currently belongs to Opus Dei.

## THE PLAZA DE LA VILLA (Town Hall Square)

This is the most beautiful medieval square in Madrid. The Town Hall is to the West, i.e., on the right of the square. It is a large baroque building, dating from 1640. It was designed by Juan Gómez de Mora, and follows the Madrid style, making use of granite from the Guardarrama mountains and red brick. The towers on the corners are imitations of those on the Palace of the Duke of Uceda, and it has a slate roof. Juan de Villanueva, the architect, built a balcony on the facade giving onto the Calle Mayor, to give a view over the procession of Corpus Christi. The decorations in the doorways and on the towers are by Teodoro Ardemans. The interior is worthy of the outside, and the building contains a painting by Goya showing "The Allegory of the City of Madrid".

The Casa de Cisneros (Cisneros' House) stands in the South side of this square. This was built by Benito Jiménez, the nephew of Cardinal Francisco Jiménez de Cisneros, during the first half of the 16th century. Its original Plateresque facade remains on Sacramento Street. It was in this house that Antonio Pérez, the famous secretary of Philip II, was imprisoned. It contains magnificent craftwork, and is currently used to hold the Mayor's office and other Town Hall departments.

The Casas de los Lujanes (The Houses of the Lujanes family) stand on the East side of the square. These are the oldest civil buildings remaining in the city, and were constructed on the orders of Álvaro de Luján. They are built in civil Mudejar style, of brick alternating with horizontal layers of rubblework (a mixture of flintstones and mortar). There is a gothic - mudejar doorway dating from 1472 which gives on to Codo Street, while the main facade is civil Castillian gothic in style, with large keystones decorated with the family shield, framed by small columns or bars in the form of an Arab arch.

The statue in the centre of the Square is of Álvaro de Bazán, the Marquis of Santa Cruz. He was the greatest mariner in Spanish history, and defeated the Turks at Lepanto and the French in the Azores. He died before the disastrous Spanish Armada occurred.

## SAN MIGUEL MARKET (on the Calle Mayor)

This stands on the spot once occupied by the Church of St. Miguel. It was built at the end of the 19th century in the ironwork architectural style then popular. It is the only one of several markets of this type remaining, and is still used as a covered market.

*Town Hall, Cisneros' house and the Lujanes' houses*

*Philip III and Mayor Square*

*General view of Mayor Square*

## THE PLAZA MAYOR (Main Square)

This used to be known as the Plaza de Arrabal. It was an irregularly shaped square surrounded by poor-looking houses with wooden supports and columns, and had been in existence from the times of Juan II of Castille. During the reign of Philip III, the Council asked Gómez de Mora to create a new Plaza here, without destroying the old Casa de la Panadería (Bakery House) which dated from 1590. They asked him to follow the model set by the square in Valladolid, which was the first regular square in Spain, and that in Lerma, which Gómez de Mora had worked on together with his uncle Francisco de Mora.

The buildings were built using brick fronted wooden frames and lead roofing. The square was inaugurated in 1620, with the celebration of the beatification of St. Isidore, which Lope de Vega worked on. 4,000 individuals lived in the houses around this square, which could hold 50,000 people.

The square suffered fires in 1631, 1672 and 1790. Juan de Villanueva was asked to undertake its definitive restoration, making important changes. It was planned to be an enclosed regular area, into which carriages would pass through rounded arches. There were columns and three floored buildings, attics and slate roofs. The square was finished in 1854, and forms a rectangle of 120 m x 94 m. The grounds occupied by the Bakery and Butchers' Buildings are in the longest sides of the rectangle.

The Plaza Mayor used to be used for all Court and social occasions, including beatifications, autos-da-fé held by the Inquisition, Royal receptions, executions, bullfights and jousts. The traditional commercial activities here were bakers' and butchers' shops, the main establishments for which used to be here, while in the 18th century the sale of textiles (clothing, silks and threads) was the main commercial activity. The shops around the Plaza currently sell souvenirs and coins, while there are also cafeterias, old inns and good restaurants.

Every Sunday morning a large fair is held in the square for the sale, purchase and exchange of coins and stamps, while during the Christmas season the centre is occupied by kiosks selling typically Christmas items.

The statue in the plaza is of Philip III, and was cast in bronze by the Italian sculptor, Juan de Bologna.

## STA. CRUZ PALACE (in the Pl. de Sta. Cruz)

This has housed the Ministry of Foreign Affairs since 1931. Building started in 1629, in the reign of Philip IV. It was designed to be the Court Prison. Designed by the baroque architect Juan Gómez de Mora, who took the Uceda Palace and Town Hall as models, it was used for legal administration, while the jail occupied the rear (the Viana or Duke of Rivas Palace). Completed in 1662, it suffered a large fire, after which it was rebuilt by Juan de Villanueva.

Its fine facade is influenced by Italian architecture, while the pediment shows an heraldic sculpture of Philip IV. Inside the building there are two large symmetrical patios, Tuscan columns and rounded arches, and a magnificent central stairway.

*Santa Cruz Palace*

## THE CHURCH OF St. ISIDORE (in Toledo Street)

The Jesuits arrived in Madrid in 1562, settling on some land in the Calle de Toledo granted to them by Leonor de Mascarenhas, Philip II's nursemaid. Empress Maria, Queen of Hungary and the sister of Carlos V, left her goods to finance building an Imperial college and Temple for the Jesuits.

Work started in 1622, to a design of Brother Sánchez, modelled on the Roman church of Il Gesú, by Vignola. It was finished in 1664 by Brother Bautista. Cross - shaped, it has a single broad nave, a dome in the centre of the transept and large baroque side chapels. The stone facade, with monumental columns and pilasters, was inspired by the facade of St. Peter's basilica. It contains statues of St. Isidore and St. Maria de la Cabeza, his wife, and two square towers.

The lantern topped dome is a typical feature of Madrid architecture, known as a "false dome". Its framework is made of wood and plaster between the interior and slate-covered outside. This feature was introduced in Madrid by Brother Bautista, and was very popular due to its low cost and lightness.

The name of this church was changed from St. Francisco Javier to St. Isidore, (patron saint of Madrid) after the expulsion of the Jesuits in 1767. In 1885 it was made Cathedral for the Madrid - Alcala diocese. It was used as such until 1993, when John Paul II consecrated the Almudena.

Damaged by fire during the civil war in 1936, it was restored. The mummified remains of St. Isidore are kept here in an urn.

*St. Isidore Cathedral*

*Night view of Puerta del Sol*

## THE SQUARE OF THE PUERTA DEL SOL

As has already been said, during medieval times Madrid was defended by walls that had been built by the Arabs. There used to be a gate in these walls here, known as the "Gate of the Sun" (Puerta del Sol). No traces of this gate exist, but this square is now the true centre of the city, and has been Kilometre One for all the Spanish roads radiating from Madrid since the times of José I Bonaparte.

Several of the best-known streets in the city start at this square. These include Arenal, Mayor, Alcalá and Montera, while the streets of Preciados and Carmen are occupied by one of the city's most important shopping centres. Sol underground station is the hub of virtually all the lines in Madrid.

The plan for the square as it is now was drawn up by Juan Bautista Peyronet in 1861. He demolished some old buildings and renovated others in a uniform style. He kept the old Post Office Building, which was designed by Marquet, a Frenchman, in 1768. This building first became the Ministry of the Interior and police headquarters, and is now used by the Presidency of the Self - Governing Region of Madrid. The people of Madrid celebrate new year's eve in this square, with the chimes of the clock on the old Post Office Building.

There is a beautiful bronze equestrian statue of Charles III between Preciados Street and Carmen Street. This reproduces a model by Pascual de Mena. There is a statue of a bear and strawberry tree, the symbol of Madrid, at the entrance to Carmen Street.

## St. FERDINAND ROYAL SCHOOL OF FINE ARTS
(13, Calle Alcalá)

*Facade of the School of Fine Arts*

Although this was a project of Philip V, it was brought into being some time after his reign, in 1752 when Ferdinand VI was on the throne. Although it was set up to train artists, it is now only used as a gallery, as fine arts are taught at the University.

The gallery was created in 1774 by Charles III. It is in the old Goyeneche Palace, which was built by José de Churriguera in 1724 and renovated in 1773 by Diego Villanueva. 1,500 paintings and 800 sculptures and engravings are stored here.

There are 18th century works by painters such as Fragonard, Giaquinto, Van Loo, Mengs, Paret, Bayeu, Tiépelo and Ranc. The collection of portraits and paintings by Goya are of especial interest.

16th century paintings held here include works by Morales, Tristán, Juan de Juanes, Tintoretto, Correggio, Bellini, Veronese, Bassano, Marinus and El Greco.

The 17th century is represented here by paintings by Rubens, Lucca Giordano, Van Dyck, Domenichino, Segheers, Vaccaro, Ribera, Zurbarán, Carreño, Caxés, Coello, Alonso Cano, Murillo and Velázquez, together with sculptures by Pedro de Mena, Ginés, Montañés and Pereira.

Paintings from the 19th century include works by Vicente López, Madrazo, González Velázquez, Esquivel, Alenza, Eugenio Lucas and Carlos Haës.

Lastly, 20th century works on show here include paintings and sculptures by artists such as Segura, Vela-Zanetti, Vaquero, Ávalos, Marés, Moreno Carbonero, Sotomayor, López-Mezquita, Martínez Cubells, Sorolla, Rosales, Pla, Benjamín Palencia, Chicharro and Picasso.

## ALCALÁ STREET

This is the longest street in Madrid. It is over 10 km long, and starts at the Puerta del Sol, leading towards Alcalá de Henares and Aragón. Palaces, convents and churches were built along this street, such as the Baroque churches of Calatrava and the Carmelite St. José de Pedro de Ribera. The St. Ferdinand Academia Real de Bellas Artes (Royal School of Fine Arts), the squares of Cibeles (Cybele) and Independencia, and the Puerta de Alcalá were built on this street during the reign of Charles III. Large palaces were built here during the 19th century, and these are now used as the head offices of several banks, such as the Banco Bilbao-Vizcaya, the Banco de Crédito and the Banco de España.

*Alcalá Street*

## PLAZA DE CIBELES (Cybele Square)

This is one of the most beautiful squares in Madrid, and is the first within the Concourse or Avenue of the Prado. The fountain of Cybele (1792) stands in the centre of the square. Cybele was the Greek goddess of farming, and was wife of Chronos and mother of Zeus. The sculpture of the goddess by Francisco Gutierrez shows her sitting in a carriage drawn by lions, which are the work of Roberto Michel.

Beautiful buildings stand around this square. The Bank of Spain stands on the corner between Alcalá and the Prado Avenue. This was built during the reign of Alfonso XII, between 1884 and 1891. It was designed by Adaro and Sainz de la Lastra, and combines neoclassical, baroque and rococo styles.

The Palace of Communications, or Post Office building, was inaugurated in 1919. It is neo-baroque in style, and its architects were Otamendi and Palacios.

*Cybele Fountain and Alcalá Gate*

Linares Palaces, now known as the Casa de America, stands between the streets of Alcalá and Recoletos. Its design shows French influence, and it was built in 1772 by Carlos Collubi.

Buenavista Palace, which is currently Army Headquarters, stands in front of Linares Palace. It was the palace of the Duchess of Alba, and has a large garden. It was built in 1777 by Juan Pedro Arnal.

Fountain of Cybele

## PASEO DEL PRADO (Prado Av.)

This is one of the most beautiful avenues of the city. It was conceived by Charles III ("The Mayor King") and the Count of Aranda as an avenue with buildings dedicated to scientific purposes. The project was drawn up in 1766 by the neoclassical baroque architects, José de Hermosilla and Ventura Rodríguez. Its layout is that of a hippodrome, with a central walkway for pedestrians and roads on each side for carriages.

The Fountain of Apollo, also known as the Four Seasons, stands between the squares of Cybele and Neptune. It was constructed in 1777, following a design by Ventura Rodríguez.

## THE NAVAL MUSEUM
(5, Paseo del Prado)

This holds a large collection of models of ships, as well as mementoes of important battles such as those of

*Fountain of Apollo*

Lepanto and Trafalgar. There are also paintings, trophies, standards, weapons and cannons. Perhaps the most interesting item is the first geographical map of America, by Juan de la Cosa.

## THE MUSEUM OF DECORATIVE ARTS (12, Montalbán)

This holds very good collections of ceramics, leather, furniture, jewellery, porcelain and all types of luxury items used in home decoration.

102

*Sword and Hat Portrait, CHURRUCA, Naval Museum*

*Fountain of Neptune*

## <u>CÁNOVAS SQUARE</u>

This is the main square in the Avenue of the Prado, and is usually known as the Plaza de Neptuno. This is because a fountain showing the God of the Sea stands in the centre of the square. This figure was designed by Ventura Rodriguez and sculpted in marble by Pascual de Mena, in 1782.

The small square to the North East is known as "Lealtad" (loyalty). It is here that the monument to the victims of the uprising against Napoleon on May 2nd stands. This is now also used as the Monument to the Unknown Soldier, and a flame is kept burning on its front. This monument was constructed from 1821 - 1840 by Isidore González Velázquez, and it takes the form of an obelisk supported by a large tomb, surrounded by the cypresses in a garden. The Stock Exchange stands behind this. It is a building in neoclassical style by Ripollés, and was built in 1848. The Ritz stands nearby. This building dates from the early years of the 20th century, and is considered to be one of the best hotels in the city, with luxurious interior decoration worthy of a palace.

## VILLAHERMOSA PALACE (in the Avenue of the Prado)

This palace stands at the North West of Cánovas Square. It was built for the widowed Duchess of Villahermoso in 1805, to a design by López Aguado. It was completely renovated by Moneo in 1989.

It is in this palace that most of the art collection of Baron Thyssen-Bornemisza is exhibited. This used to be held in Lugano, Switzerland, in Villa Favorita, and currently belongs to the Spanish State, following purchase in 1993.

This is one of the finest private collections of paintings in the world. It contains almost 800 works, with examples from all schools, and works by major painters from medieval times (1200) up to the most modern tendencies. The collection of 19th century impressionist paintings is especially fine, especially as beforehand few such works were on show in Madrid. The collection of 20th century works is unique.

*Villahermosa Palace*

## THE PLAZA DE LAS CORTES (Congress Square)

This interesting small square lies close to Cánovas Square, to which it is joined by the street named "Carrera de S. Jeronimo". The best building here is the Congress of Representatives, the construction of which started in 1882 during the reign of Isabel II. It is neoclassical in style, and was designed by Pascual Colomer. It is possibly the finest public building in Madrid, after the Royal Palace. It was built on the site once occupied by the Convent of the Holy Spirit, which had been used for holding the Cortes or Parliament from 1834 to 1841.

The facade has large columns with Corinthian capitals and a classical triangular pediment with bas-reliefs representing Spain and the Constitution. Bronze lions stand at each side of the stairs.

There is a statue Miguel de Cervantes, the famous writer, in the centre of this square.

*Palace of the Congress of Representatives*

106 *Facade of Prado Museum*

32 106

## THE PRADO MUSEUM (Paseo del Prado)

This building is the most beautiful of those from the neo-classical period in Madrid. It was built in 1785, during the reign of Charles III, by Juan de Villanueva. Of granite and brick, it was designed as the Museum of Natural Sciences, and is close to the Botanical Gardens. It was damaged in the War of Independence against Napoleon in 1808, and after being restored at King Ferdinand VII's behest in 1819, was turned into the Royal Museum of paintings.

It is one of the most important art galleries in the world, with more than five thousand paintings, engravings, drawings and sculptures. Practically all schools of painting are represented here, from medieval times to the end of the eighteenth century. Most of the Spanish monarchs were great collectors of paintings, above all Charles V, Philip II and Philip IV of the Hapsburg dynasty and Philip V, Charles III and Charles IV of the Bourbon dynasty.

Of course, the museum is unique in the world for its Spanish paintings. All the important painters are represented, together with almost all of their best works.

*Gentleman with his hand on his chest, EL GRECO*

## EL GRECO

Doménico Theotocopuli was born on the Island of Crete in 1541, where he painted icons on panels with his father. He was an apprentice for five years under Titian in Venice, and it was there the Italians called him "Greco". From Venice he moved to Rome, where he saw classical works and received his first commission from Canon Diego de Castilla, for the monastery of Saint Domingo el Antiguo in Toledo.

He is considered a Spanish artist because from 1577 to his death in 1614, he was continuously "in love" with Toledo. All his works were painted in that city, and it is there the most important ones are kept. Many of the artist's paintings in the Prado Museum come from the churches, palaces and convents of Toledo. He is a painter of the mystical, and the main characteristics of his work are the elongation of the figures, by means of which El Greco tried to represent the ascension of the soul towards God; the feminine hands with very long fingers (sometimes the middle ones are joined); and bright colours appropriate to the Venetian school, which, under the influence of the Spanish school and the baroque, grew darker as his life progressed.

More than thirty of his works are exhibited in the Prado, many on religious subjects, among which the "Trinity", from his first period in Spain, and the "Adoration of the Shepherds" as well as several portraits of Toledan nobles stand out. Among the latter is his major work "The Gentleman with his Hand on his Chest".

*Las Meninas, or the Family of Philip IV,* VELÁZQUEZ

*Vulcan's Forge, VELÁZQUEZ*

## DIEGO DE SILVA Y VELAZQUEZ

Velázquez was the greatest genius of the Spanish baroque, and a great master in the treatment of light. He was born in Seville in 1599, and died in Madrid in 1660. He studied in Seville under Herrera "The Elder" and Pacheco, whose daughter he married. At the age of twenty four he became Court Painter to Philip IV, and lived and worked in the Royal Palace of the Hapsburgs until his death. Commissioned by Philip IV, he travelled twice to Italy to buy works of art to decorate palaces and to study the great classical masters.

He is the great realistic painter, almost a realist photographer, painting what he saw and as he saw it with an enormous mastery of draughtsmanship and, above all, of light.

The museum holds more than 50 of his works, the bulk of his production, and all of them are exceptional. Many of his paintings are portraits of Philip IV and of his family, among them his masterpiece "The Ladies-in-Waiting" (Las Meninas), portraits of Philip IV's family, works with religious subjects such as "Christ on the Cross", mythological subjects such as "The Forge of Vulcan" or "The Spinners", historical subjects such as "The Surrender of Breda" and his incredible impressionistic landscapes of the Villa Médicis in Rome.

*The Surrender of Breda, VELAZQUEZ*

The Spanish baroque is also represented by more than fifty works of José de Ribera who was born in Játiva (Valencia), studied under Caravaggio and lived for many years in Naples. He was a great master of chiaroscuro techniques, and notable among his works is "The Martyrdom of Saint Bartholemew". Bartolomé Esteban Murillo who was born and lived in Seville, has more than forty paintings in the museum, including his well-known "The Immaculate Ones" and Francisco de Zurburán, the great specialist in painting the white of religious habits is represented by his intriguing mystical visions.

*The Family of Charles IV, GOYA*

## FRANCISCO DE GOYA Y LUCIENTES

Goya is perhaps the greatest Spanish painter, and is the father of many modern tendencies. Born in Fuendetodos (Zaragoza), he began to study painting in Zaragoza with the Luzán brothers and, while very young, came to Madrid where he studied with the Aragonese Bayeu brothers. He was rejected twice by the Royal Academy of Fine Arts of San Ferdinand in the competition to obtain a grant for study in Rome. In 1771 he travelled independently to Italy, and in Parma learned the technique of painting in fresco. On his return from Italy, he painted the vault of the cupola of the Basilica del Pilar. He returned to Madrid where he married Josefa Bayeu, sister of the painters Ramón and Francisco. In 1774 he was commissioned by Antonio Rafael Mengs to paint popular scenes as patterns for tapestry weaving at the Royal Tapestry Factory of Santa Bárbara. Especially notable among these are "The Pottery Dealer", "The Injured Builder", "Dance on the Banks of the Manzanares" and "Snowfall".

In 1776 he began to paint portraits of the royal family and gradually became the portraitist most sought-after by the court and the nobility. "The Family of Charles IV", "The Family of the Duke and Duchess of Osuna", "Jovellanos" and, above all, "The Clothed Maja" and "The Naked Maja" are outstanding among his portraits. He painted three Spanish Kings, Charles III, Charles IV and Ferdinand VII.

Owing to an illness, Goya became deaf and remained, during the War of Independence against Napoleon, in Madrid and at his country house called "Quinta del Sordo" (Deaf Man's Villa). Here he covered the walls with his incredible black paintings, the product of his reveries. His engravings "The Horrors of War" date from this period, as do "Caprices".

After the war, he painted his impressive historical works "The second of May" in 1808 and "The Executions at Moncloa". Sick, tired and perhaps disillusioned by the absolutist regimen of Ferdinand VII he went into voluntary exile at Bordeaux (France), where he painted his last works, including the portrait of his friend Muguiro and "The Milkmaid of Bordeaux", and there he died in 1828.

Goya was one of the most prolific painters of all times, painting kings, nobles, artists, bull-fighters, the public at large and people of all social classes.

The Prado Museum boasts the best collection of Goya works in the world, with more than one hundred and ten paintings and fifty drawings.

## FLEMISH PAINTING

In the fifteenth century, via Medina del Campo, a huge quantity of paintings and religious triptychs painted in the Netherlands was traded in Castile. The Catholic Monarchs were very fond of Flemish painting and later, owing to the legacy of the Hapsburgs, Charles V, Philip II, Philip III and Philip IV, they became the rulers of the Netherlands. The result of this is that Spain and the Museum have one of the finest collections of Flemish painting in the world. This includes magnificent paintings by Van Eyck, Roger Van der Weyden (The Descent), Hans Memling, the Master of Flemalle, Roberto Campin, the best works of Hieronymus Bosch (Philip II's favourite painter), such as "The Garden of Earthly Delights", and Pieter Brueghel the Elder.

In the seventeenth century, when *Peter Paul Rubens* came to Spain as an ambassador, Philip IV bought a large quantity of his and his students' paintings. The museum has more than eighty of Rubens' works, including some magnificent portraits and, above all, representations of mythological subjects such as "The Three Graces". Jordaens and Anthony Van Dyck are very well represented in the museum, and there are also works by Snyders, Rembrandt ("Self-portrait"), Teniers and Wouwerman.

*Self - Portrait, DURERO*

*Descent from the Cross, ROGER VAN DER WEYDEN*

 *The Firing Squads of May 3rd, GOYA*

*The Annunciation, FRA ANGELICO*

## ITALIAN PAINTING

The greater part of the Prado collection belonged to Charles V, Philip II and to Philip IV who commissioned Velázquez to buy works of art on his journeys to Italy. Charles V considered Titian to be the best painter of his time and appointed him as his official portraitist; works of his to be found in the collection are "Portrait of Charles V after the Battle of Mühlberg", and the portrait "Elizabeth of Portugal". Paintings from the Venetian school include unique works by Titian, Tintoretto, Veronese, Bassano, Giorgione, Palma and Tiepolo.

Exceptional works are Fra Angelico's Annunciation altarpiece and "The Dormition of the Virgin" by Andrea Mantegna. Raphael is very well represented by religious paintings and the superb "Portrait of a Cardinal". Works of great interest by Boticelli, Andrea del Sarto and Correggio are to be found in the museum.

There is also a good selection of French painting, above all of the Bourbon period, with works by Rigaud, Michael Van Loo, Ranc, Poussin, Watteau and Lorraine. The English school is represented by Reynolds, Romney, Lawrence and Gainsborough, and the German school by Cranach, Holbein and Albrecht Dürer with his "Self-portrait".

*The Cardinal, RAPHAEL*

*Isabel of Portugal, TITIAN*

## BUEN RETIRO MANSION

This small palace was built by Alonso de Carbonel, the architect, in the 17th century, close to the Palace of Buen Retiro which was used by Philip IV. It was used by the Court for celebrations or spectacles held for royal weddings, baptisms and the reception of foreign dignitaries. Plays were put on and firework displays were held here. During the reign of the last of the Hapsburgs, Charles II, the great Neapolitan painter Lucca Giordano created the magnificent fresco in the central hall, showing "The Allegory of the institution of the Order of the Golden Fleece". This building was remodelled in 1886 by Mariano Cardedera and Ricardo Velázquez Bosco, and was used as a topographical laboratory and stables by Alfonso XII.

*Buen Retiro Palace, seen from the Fountain of Neptune*

This building currently forms a part of the Prado Museum. It holds a fine exhibition of 19th century paintings and sculpture, from the neoclassical, romantic and impressionist periods. The collection of very large paintings by Academicians and Romantic painters of the 19th century is unique.

There are works of sculpture by Álvarez Cubero, Mariano Benlliure, José Llimona, Barba, Cánova, Thorwalsen, Vallmitjana, Blay and Querol, and paintings by Vicente López (one of the best portrait painters of the 19th century) as well as works by Raimundo and Federico de Madrazo, Ferrant, Carlos Luis Ribera, Antonio Maria Esqivel, Eugenio Lucas, Valeriano Bécquer, Genaro Pérez Villamil, Carlos Haes, Jaime Morera, Mariano Fortuny, Eduardo Rosales, Palmaroli, Pinazo, Sorolla, Russiñol and Beruete.

*Fresco by Giordano, in Buen Retiro Palace*

## ROYAL ACADEMY OF THE SPANISH LANGUAGE (Felipe IV, Academia)

Work on this building started in 1891, according to a neoclassical design by Miguel Aguado, on a site next to the Monastery of St. Jerónimo el Real. It was built to house the Corporation founded in 1713 by Philip V to work for the preservation and correct usage of the Spanish language.

## SAN JERONIMO EL REAL (Ruiz de Alarcón)

This church stands behind the Prado Museum. It formed a part of a monastery belonging to the order of the Hieronymites, founded in 1503 and almost destroyed by French troops under Murat in 1808. After being used for several purposes, the church was restored on the orders of King consort Francisco of Assisi, the husband of Isabel II, according to a neogothic design by Narciso Pascual Colomer. The investment ceremonies of the Princes of Asturias, as heirs to the throne, used to be held in this church from the times of Philip II to the reign of Isabel II. The grandparents of King Juan Carlos, Alfonso XIII and Victoria Eugenia of Battenberg, were married in this church in 1906.

*The Royal Academy of the Spanish Language*

The remains of the cloisters of the old monastery stand next to the church. This monastery was in Renaissance style, and was built by Miguel Martínez in 1612.

*The Church of St. Jeronimo el Real*

*Army Museum*

### THE ARMY MUSEUM (Mendez Nuñez, 1)

This museum was founded in 1803 by order of Manuel Godoy, the favourite of Maria Luisa of Parma and the prime minister of Charles IV. It occupies the North wing of the old palace of Buen Retiro. This palace was built in 1629 on the orders of the Count Duke of Olivares for King Philip IV, to a design by Alonso de Carbonel. Most of this palace was destroyed by Napoleonic troops. The Hall of Kingdoms, for which Velázquez painted some of his equestrian portraits and historical works, survived.

The museum holds armour, flags, standards, weapons of all types, military trophies, the portraits of military leaders, uniforms and medals. The tent used by Emperor Charles V is of great interest, as is the section on the Spanish Civil War (1936 - 1939).

### RETIRO PARK (Alfonso XII)

This has its origins in the gardens of the Buen Retiro palace, which belonged to Philip IV. There used to be a Tudor style palace here, built by Philip II for his second wife, Mary Tudor the Queen of England, daughter of Henry VIII and Catalina of Aragon.

This is the most beautiful park in Madrid, and is also the most important one in the city in historic and artistic terms.

It is in the city centre, is 120 hectares in size, and contains more than 15,000 trees. Iron railings run around the entire park, from which motor traffic is banned. There are several different entrances to this park.

There is an artificial lake at the centre of the park. Next to this is a large monument by Mariano Benlliure, the sculptor, dedicated to King Alfonso XII. There is also the "Artichoke Fountain", by Ventura Rodríguez. There are many monuments to writers, poets and military men in this park. Bellver's monument to "The Fallen Angel" should also be mentioned. This stands on the site of the old Buen Retiro Royal Porcelain Factory.

*The Monument to Alfonso XII and the lake, Retiro Park*

Two fine Exhibition Galleries stand in the park. The Crystal Palace is a pavilion made of glass on an iron frame. It was designed by Ricardo Velázquez Bosco and Alberto Palacio in 1887, as a greenhouse for exotic plants brought over from the Philippines. The other Gallery is the Palace of Velázquez, which was built by Ricardo Velázquez for the Mining Exhibition of 1883.

Many of the inhabitants of Madrid come to this park, especially at weekends. There are often painters, puppet shows, theatre and musicians to be seen in the park, and it is a fine place to go for a drink in one of its many open air bars.

*Observatory*

## THE ASTRONOMICAL OBSERVATORY

Standing in Retiro Park, close to Atocha square, this is one of the most beautiful buildings in Madrid, and is the architectural masterwork of Juan de Villanueva. It is topped by a small circular temple, with Ionic capitals, and the portico is supported by columns with Corinthian capitals.

## THE BOTANICAL GARDENS (Plaza Murillo)

Created in 1781 by Carlos III, and once one of the finest gardens in Europe, it is surrounded by iron railings, with two granite gates onto the Prado Museum and Avenue designed by Juan de Villanueva. It covers 70,000 square metres, and once held more than 30,000 different species of plants. It has a valuable collection of "dead" plants, a magnificent library, and more than 6,000 plates by the botanist and priest Celestino Mutis. These quiet gardens are not much visited.

## CHARLES V or ATOCHA SQUARE

The railway station of Atocha (1888 - 1892) was one of the first iron and glass buildings in Madrid, and was designed by Alberto Palacio. Renovated in 1991 when a building by Rafael Moneo was added, the old station now holds a beautiful tropical garden. It is one of the most important transport hubs in the city, with train, underground and the high speed rail link (AVE) to Seville.

*Atocha Station*

## THE REINA SOFIA CENTRE OF MODERN ART (Santa Isabel, 52)

This occupies a magnificent building constructed in 1781 by the Italian architect Francisco Sabatini, during the reign of Charles III. It used to be Madrid general hospital. It is baroque in style, and shows the influence of Herrera and the Escorial. Restoration started in 1980, and it was opened as an Art Centre in 1986. In 1990 it became the National Museum of Modern Art.

At 12,505 m², the exhibition area is greater than that of the MOMA (New York) (8,100 m2) or the Tokyo Museum of Modern Art (6,000 m2), and is comparable in size to the Pompidou Centre. This is a computer controlled building, with a central computer to control temperature, humidity, lighting and security alarms. The exterior lifts are an interesting feature, going up and down in glass towers.

The first, third and fourth floors are used for temporary exhibitions, while the second is given over to the permanent exhibition, otherwise known as the Spanish Museum of Modern Art.

The development of 20th century art to date may be seen here. There are works by Zuloaga, Nonell, Solana, Anglada Camarasa and Iturrino. The avant gard of the 20's and 30's is represented by works of Julio González, Juan Gris, Maria Blanchard, Gargallo and Picasso. The "Paris school" is also represented with works by Bores, Cossio, Benjamin Palencia, Viñes and Vázquez Diaz. There are surrealist works by Dali, Miró and Togores, together with others by abstract informalists such as Chillida, Chirino, Canogar, Torner, Ribera, Mompó, Saura, Viola, Millares, Lucio Muñoz, Zobel, Guerrero, Rueda, Pablo Serrano and Tapies.

The most important work held by the museum is of course "Guernica". This was painted by Pablo Picasso in Paris, from May 1st to June 4th, 1937, for the Spanish Pavilion in the Paris International Exposition. He painted it at the request of the Spanish government, and the painting shows the horrors and barbarous nature of war. There is the fall of Malaga, mothers holding their dead children, machine gunned from the air while they tried to escape down the road to Motril. The destruction of the defenseless Basque town of Guernica by the German Condor legion is shown. This painting occupies a special place in the world of art, as a terrible symbol of war and human madness. The preparatory sketches for this work are also on display. These are especially fine, as nobody used a pencil to draw with such expressive force since the time of Leonardo.

*Guernica, PICASSO*

## PABLO RUIZ PICASSO

The greatest genius to arise in painting during the 20th century was born in Malaga, Spain, in 1881. His father was a painter, and taught in the Malaga School of Fine Arts. He was transferred to La Coruña in 1891, where Picasso started to paint. In 1895 he was moved again, this time to Barcelona. It was here that Picasso painted his first large academic pictures, before going to Madrid in 1897 to study in the St. Ferdinand School of Fine Arts. He did not stay there long, and although he returned to Barcelona he soon went on to Paris, in 1900. It was here that he started painting in the style of his "blue period", until 1904 when the "Pink period" commenced. This lasted until 1906, when he initiated Cubism with "Les Demoiselles d'Avignon". This style was developed further by Braque and Juan Gris.

Picasso experimented continuously with new ideas. By 1925 he was considered to be a surrealist, and painted "Guernica" in 1937. He was an untiring worker, and produced an enormous quantity of paintings, drawings, engravings, sculptures and ceramic works. He died in 1973, in Mougins (France) at the age of ninety two.

*Alcalá Gate*

## <u>THE PLAZA DE LA INDEPENDENCIA</u> (Independence Square)

This square is located between the districts of Recoletos, Salamanca and Retiro. It is dedicated to the victory in the war against Napoleon, which lasted from 1808 to 1813. One of the park gates of the Retiro opens onto this square, in the centre of which the famous Alcalá Gate stands. This is a symbol of the city, and is the most beautiful monumental arch in Europe.

This arch was built to a design by the Italian Francisco Sabatini, to commemorate the arrival of Charles III in Madrid from Naples. Construction lasted from 1769 to 1778. It used to mark the city limits, at the point where the road to Alcalá de Henares began. The famous university founded by Cardinal Francisco Jiménez de Cisneros in 1499 is in Alcalá.

The arch is built of limestone and granite, and is composed of three central rounded arches and side arches with headpieces. It is decorated with 10 Ionic style columns, while over the central arch there is a commemorative plaque and a great shield. The decoration consisting of children with military trophies is the work of Roberto Michel y Gutierrez.

## THE PLAZA DE COLON (Columbus Square)

This square lies between Recoletos and Castellana avenues, at the edge of the quarter of Salamanca. It dates from the 19th century, and was completely renovated in 1977. There is a large car park under this square, together with the airport bus terminal and Madrid Cultural Centre, with a theatre and an exhibition hall.

The neo-Gothic monument to Columbus dating from 1886 by Arturo Mélida is the oldest feature of this square. The Gardens of the Discovery are on the East side of this square, where the Mint used to stand. The large sculptures on the theme of the discovery of America are by Vaquero Turcios. The "Columbus Towers" on the North West side of this square were designed by Antonio Lamela. They were built from the top downwards.

## THE WAX MUSEUM (Centro Colón)

This opened in 1972, and is now one of the finest in Europe. It contains images of more than 300 famous people, and also has displays of famous crimes and others containing horror shows.

*Monument to Columbus, and the Columbus Towers*

125

*National Library*

## THE NATIONAL LIBRARY (Paseo de Recoletos, 20)

This is housed in a building known as the Palace of Libraries and Museums, which was opened in 1892. The original design for this building was by F. Jareño, and it was finished by Ruiz Salces in neoclassical style. There is an impressive stairway in the main facade, and large corinthian columns topped by a pediment decorated with sculptures by Agustín Querol.

This is one of the best libraries in the world, and contains almost two million books, including approximately 2,500 from before the year 1500.

## THE ARCHEOLOGICAL MUSEUM (Serrano, 13)

This was set up in 1867 by Isabel II, and it was moved into the current building in 1895. It holds a large exhibition of historical artifacts, from prehistorical times to the 19th century.

A reproduction of the Altimira caves in Santander has been constructed in the garden of the museum. The paintings in these caves constitute one of the most important paleolithic finds in Europe.

The museum contains masterworks of Iberian culture, such as the figures of the "Lady of Elche" (5th century BC) the "Lady of Baza" (4th century BC) and the "Offering Lady", from Cerro de los Santos (Albacete). It also holds several Iberian gold treasures, and the votive Visigoth crowns of Guarrazar from the 8th century, as well as Egyptian, Greek, Roman and Arab sculptures.

*The Lady of Baza*

*The Lady of Elche*

*Salesas Reales Church*

# THE CHURCH OF THE SALE-SAS REALES (Bárbera de Braganza)

This church used to form part of a monastery, and is now the parish church of St. Bárbara. It is one of the most typical examples of Bourbon baroque architectural style in a public building. This monastery was founded by Bárbara de Braganza, the wife of Ferdinand VI, as a school for the education of the daughters of the nobility, and also to be her residence in the case of her being widowed.

Building work started in 1750, to a design by the French architect, Francisco Carlier, and it was finished in 1757. It cost so much (more than 80 million reales) that a popular saying at the time was "Barbara Queen, barbarous taste: barbarous work, barbarous expense". The Spanish architect Francisco Moradillo also collaborated in the design of the building, changing the towers on the facade, the second level of the church and its dome. Following dissolution the convent became the Law Courts, while the church was used by the parish.

The church, which is in the form of a cross, is magnificently decorated in different types of marble, while the dome and supporting arches were painted al fresco by González Velázquez. There is a painting of the Visitation by F. Mura on the high retable, and the sculptures and relief work are by Olivieri. The retables in the transepts hold paintings by Cignaroli (The Holy Family) and Giaquinto (St. Francisco de Sales and St. Juana de Chantal).

The transept also holds the tombs of Ferdinand VI (designed by Sabatini) and General O'Donnell, by Suñol the sculptor. The tomb of Queen Bárbara of Braganza stands in the sanctuary, and is the work of Olivieri.

*Salesas Reales Church*

*Municipal Museum (main facade). Old hospice.*

## THE MUNICIPAL MUSEUM (Fuencarral, 78)

The old hospice has housed this museum since 1929. It is one of the finest examples of Madrid baroque style. It was founded in 1673 by Queen Mariana of Austria, and was known as the Hospice of Ave Maria and St. Ferdinand. The chief architects during construction from 1673 to 1703 were Aredemans, Arroyo and Philip Sánchez. Lucca Giordano painted the work "St. Ferdinand before the Virgin" which presides over the church.

The Marquis of Vadillo requested Pedro de Ribera to construct the main facade, the doorway of which has become famous, in 1721. Work on this lasted until 1726, and it is one of the finest examples of decorated baroque.

This is a very interesting museum, in which the way the city has grown may be seen and studied. There are archeological remains, paintings, drawings, photographs, craft works in precious metals, porcelain and furniture. A painting of the "Virgin and Child" by Pedro de Berruguete stands out, as does "The Allegory of the City of Madrid", by Goya, and a model of the city made in 1830 by León Gil de Palacio.

The Municipal Library is also housed in this building.

## THE MUSEUM OF ROMANCE (San Mateo, 13)

This was founded in 1924 by the Marquis de Vega-Inclan. It is housed in the small palace built by Manuel Martínez Rodríguez for General Marquis de Matallana, in 1779.

The museum is a perfect expression of the romantic atmosphere of the 19th century, especially the times of Ferdinand VII and Isabel II, and contains furniture, portraits, clocks, paintings and books. The art collection is especially interesting, and contains works by great artists of the period, including Goya, Vicente López, Mengs, Pérez Villaamil, Alenza, Esquivel and Valeriano Bécquer.

The museum also has a room dedicated to the great writer and journalist Mariano José de Larra "Figaro". He was a typical representative of the romantic period, and the room contains his personal effects and the pistol which he used to kill himself, when the woman he loved left him.

*Museum of Romance*

*Into the Water, SOROLLA*

## THE SOROLLA MUSEUM (Paseo General Martínez Campos, 37)

This is housed in the last building in Madrid to be lived in by the painter Sorolla, and it also contains his studio. The house and the collection of paintings and mementoes of the artist were donated in 1925 by his widow, Clotilde García del Castillo.

Joaquín Sorolla y Bastida was born in Valencia, in 1863. He studied painting at Valencia School of Fine Art, and lived for a while on a grant in Rome before going on to Paris, where he made contact with the contemporary art world. He won prizes at exhibitions in Munich, Chicago, Paris, Berlin and Vienna. He was the colourist painter of the light of Eastern Spain. He was the most popular portrait painter in Madrid at the end of the 19th century, and from 1911 to 1919 painted the mural decorations of the library of the Hispanic Society of America, New York. He died in Cercedilla (Madrid) in 1923.

The museum holds many of his paintings, together with some of his family portraits.

## LÁZARO GALDIANO MUSEUM (Serrano, 122)

This is housed in a small palace known as "Parque Florido". The museum was the creation of José Lazaro Galdiano, a businessman, who left his collections and treasures to the Spanish state on his death in 1947.

This magnificent museum contains exceptional collections of medieval and renaissance enamels (some of which are signed by Penicaud) together with ivory, weapons, armour, fans, jewellery, ecclesiastical decorations, furniture, coins and crystal items, such as the famous glass of Emperor Rudolf II. There is also a fine collection of paintings, including the only painting by Leonardo da Vinci in Madrid (The Saviour), early Flemish works, the self - portrait of Pedro de Berruguete, several works by El Greco, the portrait of Saskia by Rembrandt, 19 works by Goya and portraits and landscapes by 19th century English painters, such as Reynolds and Gainsborough. All schools of art are represented here.

*The Lazero Galdiano Museum*

*Ventas Bullring (also known as the Monumental)*

## THE BULL RING (Alcalá, Ventas underground station)

This bullring is known as "The Monumental" or "Ventas". It is the largest in Spain, and can hold 23,000 spectators. It is known as "the Cathedral" of the whole world of bullfighting. Bullfighters are not thought to be fully qualified until they have performed here, and the antiquity of bull breeders is dated from the time their bulls first appear in this ring.

The bullring was built in 1929. It is by Anibal González in neomudejar style, in brick with horseshoe arches and ceramic decorations.

Bullfights are held here every Sunday and holiday from March to the end of October. The festival of St. Isidore (patron saint of Madrid) is celebrated every May, when the best matadors take part in bullfights every day for three weeks.

A Museum of Bullfighting was opened here in 1951. Amongst other curios, there are bullfight posters, bullfighters' costumes, capes, swords, banderillas and pieces of harness belonging to famous bullfighters (Guerrita, Granero, Joselito, Belmonte, Manolete and El Cordobés). There are also the heads of famous bulls, with portraits, busts and other mementoes of bullfighters.

## PASEO DE LA CASTELLANA (Castellana Avenue)

This avenue already existed at the end of the nineteenth century, and several small palaces dating from that period can still be found on it. It begins at Plaza de Colón and stretches for 7 kilometres, reaching beyond the Plaza de Castilla. It is the most spacious and most beautiful avenue in the modern part of the city. The evolution of the city throughout this century can be seen clearly in its magnificent buildings, most of which are ultra-modern. The most interesting buildings are described below:

The **UNION Y FÉNIX BUILDING** (Castellana, 37). Built in 1971 by Gutierrez Soto, it features several pavilions which are set parallel and perpendicular to Castellana Avenue.

The outdoor Museum of abstract sculpture is located below the overhead walkway between Serrano and Eduardo Dato, near to the United States Embassy. It was inaugurated in 1972 and has works of interest by Julio González, Ribera, Subirachs, Sobrino, Leoz, Gabino and, most striking of all, Chillida's six-ton sculpture "El Encuentro" (The Meeting), suspended from the structure of the bridge.

The **BANKUNION BUILDING** (Castellana, 46). Built in 1975 by Corrales and Vázquez Molezún, this is, both conceptually and formally, one of the most original buildings in the Paseo.

The **COMPAÑIA DE SEGUROS CATALANA DE OCCIDENTE BUILDING** (Plaza Emilio Castelar). Designed by Raphael de la Hoz in 1988, it consists of one prism placed off centre upon another.

A monument to the renowned politician, Emilio Castelar, president of the First Republic between 1873 and 1874, stands in the centre of the square. It is the work of Mariano Benlliuro.

*Nuevos Ministerios (New Ministries) (main facade)*

The **CAIXA BUILDING** (Castellana, 61) It was built in 1978 by Bosch Aymerich in the form of an inverted pyramid, with the floors folding one above another towards the centre in the direction of the base.

In the centre of St. John of the Cross Plaza, which is dedicated to the famous sixteenth century mystic, there is a luminous fountain designed by Buigas. The monument to the Spanish Constitution of 1978 and another one dedicated to Isabella the Catholic, designed by Manuel Oms, stand in gardens next to the square, in the right-hand slip road of the Castellana. Behind the gardens, upon a hill, stands the Museum of Natural Sciences, (Castellana 84), which was created in 1911. It houses a magnificent collection of meteorites and minerals, as well as desiccated mammals, insects, molluscs and fossils.

**NUEVOS MINISTERIOS** (Castellana, on the corner of St. John of the Cross Plaza). This is a granite building on which work was started by the architect Zuazo between 1932 and 1936, on land which had been occupied by the former hippodrome. This first phase followed the Herrerian architectural model as exemplified in the Escorial Monastery, with a predominance of straight lines. It was finished between 1940 and 1942 by García Lomas, Torroja and Rodríguez Cano. On the side facing the St. John of the Cross Plaza, there is a bronze statue of General Francisco Franco on horseback, the only one in Madrid.

After the Raimundo Fernández Villaverde crossing, the extension of the Paseo de la Castellana begins, which used to be called the Avenida del Generalissimo Franco. It was built after the civil war of 1936-39.

The most futuristic area of the city and its most important business centre is the large space called AZCA, between the Paseo de la Castellana, Raimundo Fernández Villaverde and General Perón. It comprises numerous "towers" or individual isolated buildings with no relation among them, which are meant to be distinct elements, each striking in its own right. They surround an area laid out with gardens in which the Plaza Picasso is to be found. The different sectors of AZCA interconnect by means of pedestrian-only galleries, while vehicles go by underground routes. There are large stores, a multi-centre with fashion and fashion accessory shops, and many restaurants and cafeterias for those who frequent or work in the complex, as well as pubs, discotheques, nightclubs and fast-food

*AZCA and General Perón street, seen from Capitan Haya Street*

outlets for young people who frequent the area by night. The most noteworthy buildings of architectural merit in the AZCA financial district are the following:

The **WINDSOR BUILDING** (Raimundo Fernández Villacerde, 65), which is 98 metres tall and was planned by Alas and Casariego in 1979 for commercial premises, shows and offices. It is a tower supported on a base formed by other buildings. The monotony of the blank wall is relieved with a mezzanine and different coloured glass.

The **BILBAO-VIZCAYA BANK BUILDING** (Castellana, 79-81) is 108 metres tall and was built by Saenz de Oiza in 1981. It is made of iron which, due to oxidation, is changing colour. Two central nuclei are supported on lintels joined by arcades under which the railway tracks pass.

The **PICASSO TOWER** (Plaza Picasso) has 44 stories and, at 157 metres, is the capital's tallest building. Built in 1988 by the Japanese architect Minoru Yamasaki, it is visible from all the ways into the city and could be the symbol of today's Madrid.

The **EUROPA TOWER** (Castellana, on the corner of General Perón) is 113 metres tall. Built by Miguel Oriol in 1987, it is original because of its visual impact, achieved by circular forms and the top of the building with its heliport.

The **CONFERENCE AND EXHIBITIONS PALACE** (Paseo de Castellana, 99) occupies a spacious site, with a square laid out with gardens which is dedicated to the artist Joan Miró who created the ceramic mural which adorns the facade of the building in 1980. It was built in 1970 by Pablo Pintado and has a double auditorium which can hold more than 3,000 participants.

The **SANTIAGO BERNABÉU STADIUM** (Castellana, on the corner of Concha Espina) belongs to the Real Madrid Club and is the most important football stadium of the city, with a capacity of 110,000 spectators. The final of the 1982 world championship, in which Italy beat Germany, was played here. It was built between 1944 and 1950 by Manuel Muñoz Monasterio and extended in 1982 by Luis Alemany. The pitch is five metres below ground level.

*Santiago Bernabeu Stadium*

*AZCA, Picasso Tower and Europa Tower*

## PLAZA DE CASTILLA

There is a fountain in the centre of the square and a monument to the politician Joaquín Calvo Sotelo, whose assassination in July, 1936 sparked off the Civil War. Also there are two extremely original leaning towers under construction for office premises. Designed by the American John Burgee, they are called Puerta de Europa (Gate of Europe) and stand at the entrance to the N-1 dual carriageway which leads to Burgos and France.

*Castilla Square (with the monument to Calvo Sotello and the KIO Towers in the background)*

## CHAMARTIN STATION (Agustín de Foxá)

This is one of the busiest and most functional stations in Europe and the capital's most important rail communications hub, being the departure point for trains bound for the north, east and south of Spain and, via connections at the French border, to the major European cities. In its commercial area there are shops, cafeterias, restaurants, a discotheque, a skating rink and a bowling alley.

## CAMPO DE LAS NACIONES

The Campo de las Naciones was inaugurated in 1992. Situated to the north-east of the city, near Barajas airport and very well-connected with the M-40, it is a great urban complex, the economic and business engine of the city's future. The new Palacio de los Congresos, designed by Ricardo Bofill, is located here together with two large hotels, an International Business Centre and all kinds of sport and leisure amenities. In fact, most trade fairs and conferences are held here.

The Juan Carlos I park, next to Campo de las Naciones, has an area of more than 2.2 million square metres and is twice the size of the Parque de Retiro. It contains gardens, wooded areas (among them the "Garden of the Three Cultures" which commemorates the past coexistence of Muslims, Jews and Christians) and the largest outdoor auditorium in Europe. There is also a stream which runs for 1,900 metres, crossed by gangways and bridges.

*Nations' Park; fountain and monument to Juan Carlos, Count of Barcelona*

## GRAN VIA

This is one of the best-known streets of the city. It links Calle Alcalá with the Plaza de España. The street itself is completely different from the district where it is situated, as it was built at the beginning of the century to facilitate communication between the east and west of the city. Houses and old buildings were pulled down to make way for it.

*Night time view of the Gran Via*

Work began in 1910, in the reign of Alfonso XIII, and the street was completed in 1950. Cinemas, cafeterias, travel agencies, air-line and maritime offices abound in Gran Vía and half way along it the Plaza del Callao marks the entrance to a major commercial zone which is perhaps the best-known in the city. This is situated in the pedestrian precincts, Preciados and Carmen, which link the Gran Vía and the square of the Puerta del Sol with its shops and department stores.

There are some beautiful buildings in Gran Vía, examples of early twentieth century architecture (pseudo-plateresque and neo-neoclassical) among which the National Telephone Company of Spain building, the Press Building (Palacio de la Prensa) and the Music Building (Palacio de la Música) are especially noteworthy. The first of these stands 81 metres tall and was built in 1926 by Ignacio de Cárdenas; it was the city's tallest building until the Madrid Tower (Torre de Madrid) was erected in the Plaza de España. The second was built by Pedro de Muguruza in 1924 and the last by Secundino Zuazo in 1925.

## PLAZA DE ESPAÑA

This square is one of the largest and most beautiful in the city centre. It is situated very near to the Royal Palace, at the end of Gran Vía and the following streets lead off from it: Bailén, Cuesta de San Vicente, Ferraz, Princesa and Reyes. In the square, there are two buildings which, until the erection of the Picasso Tower (Torre de Picasso) in the AZCA complex, were the tallest in Madrid. The 117-metre Spain Building (Edificio de España) comprising apartments, offices and a hotel, is also to be found here. It was built by the Otamendi brothers towards the end of the 1940's. The Torre de Madrid, by the same architects, was built in 1952 on the corner of Princesa Street. It is 130 metres tall, has 32 floors and consists of offices and apartments.

A monument to the author of "Don Quixote", Miguel de Cervantes Saavedra, who died in Madrid in 1616, stands in the centre of the square surrounded by olive trees from

the region of La Mancha. The monument was made in the 1920's by the sculptor Coullaut Valera and there are bronze statues of Don Quixote of La Mancha and his squire, Sancho Panza in front of it. Around the monument, in addition to Miguel de Cervantes himself, the writer's main fictional characters are represented.

At the head of calle Ferraz stands the carmelite church of St. Joseph and St. Teresa, which was built in the last century. Neo-byzantine in style, it has an interesting cupola adorned with mosaics.

*Spain Square*

## THE CERRALBO MUSEUM (Calle Ventura Rodríguez, 17)

The museum is installed in a small palace built in 1893 by Alejandro Sureda and Luis Cabello as the residence of Don Enrique de Aguilera y Gamboa (1845-1922), XVII marquis of Cerralbo and the museum's founder. The marquis was a poet, man of letters, archeologist and a great art collector. Inside, there are frescos, furniture and paintings of the founder's times, as well as paintings by El Greco, Herrera, Antolínez, Ribera, Zurbarán, Alonso Cano, Meléndez, Vicente López, Snyders, Mengs, Eugenio Lucas, Tiépolo, Reni, Murillo and a terracotta work by Andrea della Robbia. There are also suits of armour, chinaware, silverware and various objects and curiosities which belonged to the founder, and a magnificent library and ballroom.

## PRINCESA STREET

This is one of the most important streets of the Argüelles district, joining the Plaza de España with the Complutense University and the radial N-VI road for the north-east. The street bears this name in honour of Princess Isabel, affectionately called "la Chata" (The Snub-Nosed), daughter of Isabel II who lived nearby and was much loved by the people of Madrid.

*Main ballroom, Cerralbo Museum*

Today, Calle Princesa is a major commercial centre with shops, department stores and cafeterias. The area suffered quite a lot of damage during the civil war and for this reason there are many new and reconstructed buildings.

## THE LIRIA PALACE (Calle Princesa)

This is the official residence of the duke and duchess of Alba, Spain's most important noble family. Built in 1773 by the neo-classicist, Ventura Rodríguez, it stands in a beautiful garden. From an artistic point of view, it is considered to be second only, in Madrid, to the Royal Palace. It is difficult to visit as a written request must be made in advance to the duke and duchess of Alba.

The palace was restored after the civil war and contains Madrid's most beautiful collection of furniture and objets d'art. There are magnificent Flemish tapestries, suits of armour, paintings and portraits by Goya, Titian (Portrait of the Duke of Alba), Mengs, Vicente López, el Greco, Ribera, Murillo, Rembrandt and a very beautiful portrait by Winterhalter of the Empress Eugenia de Montijo.

*Liria Palace (main facade)*

*Triumphal Arch*

## <u>TRIUMPHAL ARCH</u> (Plaza Moncloa)

Built in 1947 at the foot of Princesa Street in the Plaza de la Moncloa to commemorate General Franco's victory in the civil war of 1936-1939, the arch marks the entrance to the Complutense University Campus. Founded in 1927 by Alfonso XIII and destroyed during the civil war, it is the largest public university in Spain, with 130,000 students.

The headquarters of the Air Force are also to be found in Plaza de la Moncloa. They were built in an architectural style imitative of the Escorial Monastery on the site which had, before the civil war, been occupied by the Model Prison.

## <u>MUSEUM OF AMERICA</u> (Plaza de Moncloa)

This was built in 1941 upon a hill at the entrance to Complutense University, next to the church of St.Thomas and the "Moncloa Lighthouse", which is an interesting vantage point over this part of the city.

The recently refurbished museum contains a reproduction of the Aztec calendar, textiles, idols and samples of Pre-Columbian and Post-Columbian South American art. Most notable are pieces from Michoacán, the incredible treasures of the Columbian "Quimbayas" in gold, stone relief work from Quixmal, low relief work from Palenque representing a seated person, and Maya codices (the "Troano" and the "Cortesino"). There is also a major collection of Mexican and Peruvian pottery and several objects of Inca art.

## PARQUE DEL OESTE

This park was created towards the end of the nineteenth century, beginning as an idea of Alberto Aguilera's. The uncultivated lands of San Bernadino were transformed into lovely walks and flower beds. The park reaches from Rosales to la Florida and from la Moncloa to the hill of Principe Pío, and has an area of 84 hectares.

In this park, in Rosales Avenue, there is the station of a cable car which passes over the valley of the river Manzanares to the Casa de Campo park. The trip takes 15 minutes and is one of the best ways to see old Madrid, including the Royal Palace, the cathedral, and the church of St. Francis. The new districts built next to the Casa de Campo can also be seen along the N-V, or Portugal, road.

The Rose gardens are extremely beautiful. Magnificent examples of roses may be found here from April to November.

There is a hill in one part of the park where the Barracks of the Mountain Troops stood before the civil war. It was destroyed by republican troops in July 1936 at the beginning of the war. On the hill is the noteworthy Egyptian temple of Debod, dating from the fourth century B.C. It is the only Egyptian temple to be found in Europe, and was brought to the park from the valley of Nubia after flooding by water from the river Nile caused by the Aswan dam. Plays and concerts are performed and exhibitions held in the temple in summer. It was a present from the government of President Nasser to General Franco, for help given by the Spanish government in moving Egyptian temples prior to the building of the Aswan dam. From the hill there is a beautiful panorama of old Madrid.

*Debod Temple, in Oeste Park*

*Fresco, GOYA, San Antonio de la Florida*

## <u>SAN ANTONIO DE LA FLORIDA</u> (Paseo S. Antonio de la Florida)

The hermitage of San Antonio is very close to the old North, or Principe Pío, railway station. The hermitage was built between 1792 and 1798 by the Italian neo-classicist, Fontana, in the reign of Charles IV. Its facade is of a single piece decorated with pilasters upon a granite plinth.

In 1798, Francisco de Goya decorated the cupola and vaults of the hermitage in fresco with incredible expressive freedom, even using a sponge to lay on colours. In these frescos he painted "The Adoration of the Holy Trinity" in the vault above the larger altar and in the cupola, "A Miracle of Saint Anthony of Padua". He finished the latter work in four months. It represents the miracle performed by Saint Anthony when he brought a murder victim back to life so that he could testify before the Tribunal of Lisbon to the innocence of his father, who was unjustly accused of murder. The saint was in Italy at this time. The people in Goya's painting are men and women of Madrid from his own time.

This Aragonese genius's mortal remains lie in a tomb in the floor of the hermitage. He died in Bordeaux in 1828 and his body was brought to Madrid in 1919. However, although his body was found when his remains were brought back, the head had been stolen.

Each year between the 12th and 21st of June one of the city's most popular street fairs is held next to the hermitage to commemorate the feast of Saint Anthony and Ash Wednesday. This is the traditional Entierro de la Sardina (Burial of the Sardine), which marks the end of the carnival, and which Goya represented magnificently in his pictures.

## SEGOVIA BRIDGE

Built over the river Manzanares between 1572 and 1588 with granite ashlars, this is the city's oldest bridge. It is situated at the foot of the hill on which the Royal Palace stands and was designed by King Philip II's architect, Juan de Herrera to substitute an old wooden bridge. It served as a link between the old Royal Palace (Alcazar) where the king worked, and the Casa de Campo, where the king went to relax. The poets remarked that it was "too much of a bridge for such a small river" (it has nine arches).

*Segovia Bridge*

## CASA DE CAMPO

Ten times larger than the famous Boulogne park in Paris, this is the biggest natural park in the city. It has an area of about 1,740 hectares and extends to the other side of the river Manzanares between the Extremadura road (N-V) and the La Coruña road (N-VI). It is surrounded by a rubblework wall.

Philip II acquired the original lands in 1553 from the Vargas family and ordered a small palace to be built near to the King's Bridge (Puente del Rey) entrance, where a statue of Philip III once stood which can be seen today in the Plaza Mayor. The land was intended for cultivation and olive plantations, and Philip II ordered it to be repopulated with different kinds of trees. Later the estate was extended and made more beautiful by Ferdinand VI, Charles III, Isabel II and María Cristina of Hapsburg, the mother of Alfonso XIII.

In 1931, the provisional government of the Second Republic authorised the handing over of what had hitherto been the Royal Casa del Campo to the people of Madrid as a public park.

This park really is the lungs of the city, and it has several entrance gates: the Río or main gate, the Castilla gate, the Medianil, the Aravaca, the la Venta and the Angel. Inside it there are curious buildings such as the Old Pheasant House, the "Little Tower", and the "Management House". There is also an artificial lake with boats, surrounded by bars and snack bars and an Amusement Park. The Zoological gardens are very well designed and their special attractions are the pandas and a magnificent dolphinarium.

Also, during the feast of Saint Isidore, in what is known as the Venta de Batán (a kind of Andalucian farm), the bulls which are going to be fought in the Las Ventas bullring are put on public display.

*The lake, Casa de Campo*

*The Zoo, Casa de Campo*